Pre-Fab Living

Avi Friedman

Pre-Fab Living

with over 220 illustrations

CONTENTS

INTRODUCTION
Pre-fabrication: Types and Methods

In rapidly changing social, environmental and economic landscapes, builders and housing authorities around the world are facing an urgent need to explore new practices in residential production. Chief among these is a renewed attention to factory-built pre-fab homes, which have the potential to address contemporary challenges of affordability and resource-efficiency.

Types and methods of pre-fabrication
Pre-fabricated units are built entirely in a factory, or with factory-produced components, before being transported to site as a single element or in parts, and then assembled.[1] There are several types of production methods:

Manufactured Also known as mobile or plug-and-play homes, built as complete units and transported to site, before being connected to utilities.

Modular Ranging from a single room to multiple units, made from factory-produced sections, then shipped to site and hoisted into place.

Panellized Produced as exterior and interior panels, provide a middle ground in the degree of finish, ease of transportation and delivery.

Timber-framed Assembled from large factory-produced wooden logs.

Kit of parts Made from sub-components that are packed and delivered as a bundle, ready for assembly.

In many countries, factory-built homes have increased their market share over conventional construction thanks to some notable advantages. Factory production takes place in a controlled environment, allowing for a more energy- and material-efficient process.[2] Damage and delays caused by unpredictable weather are eliminated, and robotically assisted labour ensures that production rate is increased, with minimal errors. With labour costs reduced, consumers benefit from both equivalent built qualities and faster delivery. But there are challenges, from inventory management and energy consumption during periods of low activity in the factory, to high delivery and installation costs.

Trends affecting pre-fab production

The 21st century has introduced a perfect storm of societal changes, which require the rethinking of old design and construction strategies. Variations occur in the manifestation of these trends worldwide, but they remain relevant and applicable to most Western nations. The economic advantages of pre-fabrication are easily measurable. In urban centres, house prices have risen sharply, making buying one's own home more difficult, particularly for seniors and young people, with the latter representing anywhere from 35 to 50 per cent of potential buyers. Recent decades have seen both increasing pressure on first-time buyers, putting many in debt just at the age when they might want to purchase a home or start a family, and a shortage of housing stock, owing to a scarcity of serviced land and the high costs of infrastructure and construction.[3]

Pre-fabrication offers a solution that is cost- and time-efficient. In a streamlined factory environment, computer-aided design (CAD) and building information modelling (BIM) software can calculate the raw materials needed to minimize waste and reduce variability of labour.[4] With the retirement of the baby-boomer generation and slower entry of young people into the job market, labour shortages will raise the cost of traditional practices. In-plant automation, however, enables work to be carried out by machines, directing manual labour towards more complex finishing processes. As rising prices lead to the

Above
On-site construction.

Previous pages
Loblolly House, USA, KieranTimberlake.

On p. 2
Floating Houses IJburg, Netherlands, Marlies Rohmer.

demand for smaller houses, mass-customization allows consumers to tailor a product that suits them financially and spatially. It also generates economic versatility by effectively lowering the cost of a home, thus attracting a wider range of consumers.

The environmental impact of a house occurs both during construction and while it is being lived in. By using an automated process, pre-fabrication effectively reduces material waste and energy consumption during construction. The factory setting allows for more convenient testing of new technologies, which also contributes to a reduction in waste and energy use. Public awareness has also increased, and new objectives and policies, including the LEED (Leadership in Energy and Environmental Design) qualification, have helped to guide innovations in building methods and act as benchmarks against which new projects are evaluated. Initiatives such as BREEAM, Energy Star and the EnerGuide rating system encourage consumers to choose and developers to build energy-efficient homes.

These trends demonstrate that previous home-building norms are changing, and that recognition of the need to develop housing prototypes that can be built in higher densities is gradually taking hold. Houses that conserve natural resources during construction and energy after occupancy are more likely to be developed and, with energy costs mounting, will appeal to both builders and consumers. Net-zero and solar-powered homes, along with the use of innovative HVAC (heating, ventilation and air-conditioning) technologies, green roofs, recycled building materials and water-efficient systems, have all increased in recent years.[5]

Greater urbanization has forced a high-density lifestyle in city centres, and the trend for smaller families, together with an aging population, parallels a growing demand for smaller, low-maintenance, affordable homes. The diversity of homebuyers has also produced a need for homes that can be tailored to the spatial requirements of each family. Pre-fabrication again offers an affordable solution by being able to produce versatile housing units.[6] It allows the mass-production of parts that can be customized, with options to upgrade as needs change.

With the population reaching the critical mass necessary to explore the alternatives set out by policy-makers, developers and architects, there has been a rise in options to accommodate a variety of households in buildings with smaller footprints, creating diversity in the housing stock.

The need for a home to adapt to changing circumstances is also important. Flexibility – the capacity of a house to provide an effective initial fit, while still being able to facilitate responses to future changes – is a pivotal issue when designing or purchasing a home. Changing needs are causing occupants to re-evaluate standard room types and their integration within the home.[7] New concepts that are being explored include aging in place, and multi-generational, small-sized and adaptable dwellings. The nature of the pre-fabrication industry's design and production methods means that it can respond to these challenges innovatively and efficiently. And with consumers re-assessing the layouts of their homes, pre-fab houses are becoming more competitive in the marketplace and gaining the interest of consumers and builders alike.

Contemporary advancements in technology have provided manufacturers with more efficient mechanisms to not only design and construct houses, but also to reach customers. The digital revolution has had a significant effect on the design industry, which has adopted the use of 3D modelling and BIM software over the last decade or so.[8] These methods allow for the simple integration of innovative designs and products, and effectively connect with the factory-manufacturing process to reduce the cost of both design and construction, making homes more affordable.

Circumstances in home-building are changing, and the demand for pre-fabricated housing will continue to rise, forcing designers, architects and manufacturers to come up with ever-more innovative solutions.

Digital and fabrication advances, including 3D-printing, have renewed the interest of designers in factory-built housing, and contemporary pre-fab homes are no longer seen as dull or technically inferior to conventionally built ones.[9] In Japan, for example, over 120,000 houses – one-third of all newly built homes – are made in the factory each year.[10] This rising trend can be attributed to the financial, environmental and structural advantages of pre-fabrication. Building in a factory setting minimizes the problems associated with vandalism, storage and delays caused by weather, and requires fewer skilled workers, so that labour costs are reduced. Another major benefit is time: an efficient, high-tech factory can produce a house in a week, whereas on-site construction, on average, takes over five months.[11]

NEW DESIGN TRENDS

Advances in pre-fabrication methods

There are several types of pre-fabricated systems, subsystems and components – with a panellized system being the most widely used – which can be combined to provide a complete system package. Nine types of panellized systems, applicable to wood-framed residential construction, can be divided into three categories.

Open-sheathed OSPs are available in almost as many variations as conventional wall construction. The most common systems have 38 × 140 mm (1½ × 5½ in.) studs with plywood or waferboard sheathing, or 38 × 89 mm (1½ × 3½ in.) studs and extruded polystyrene sheathing. In either case, panels are delivered open to the interior to allow for the installation of electrics and/or plumbing. Batt insulation is usually installed on site, and is sometimes supplied by the manufacturer.

Structural sandwich SIPs, or foam-core panels, comprise a core of rigid foam insulation, which is laminated between two facing materials. The core material, containing pre-cut electrical chases, may be one of four types of insulation: moulded bead expanded polystyrene; extruded polystyrene; polyurethane or polyisocyanurate. A variety of options are available for the joints between the panels.

Unsheathed structural USPs, or composite panels, comprise wood or metal structural elements combined with rigid foam insulation infill, usually expanded polystyrene. Four basic variations of this system are available, with different configurations for the structural elements, which provide a continuous thermal break and/or air space on the interior of the panel.

For each system, it is possible to 'add value' to the panel by integrating a larger portion of the building envelope during fabrication. Added components vary from air barriers to exterior and/or interior finishes. The extent to which the panels are finished has different implications for the build team. One of the significant advantages of pre-fab panel systems is the superior quality achieved through the manufacturing process, measured by craftsmanship, technical performance and durability. A system's craftsmanship governs its potential to achieve consistent levels of performance from one application to another. Its technical performance, particularly with respect to air-tightness, will affect the rate of deterioration owing to condensation.

Unsheathed structural panels provide a good performance in all respects, but benefit from a few extraordinary characteristics. Their biggest advantage is that they can overcome the inadequate workmanship that can be found in conventional construction without resorting to unfamiliar building techniques. The use of expanded polystyrene foam between the structural elements significantly improves the performance of the

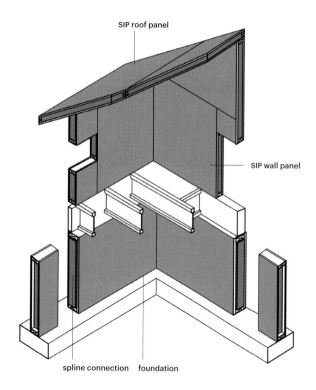

SIP roof panel

SIP wall panel

spline connection   foundation

3D-printing and automated production

3D-printing – the production of physical objects, layer by layer, using automated computer-controlled machines – promises to be the next breakthrough in pre-fabrication. The most common printers are gantry-type systems, which were developed for additive manufacturing; other methods include cable-suspended printing heads and small robots, to name a few. The chosen method usually depends on the material used. The process is still in an incubation stage, but is being developed rapidly to produce structures with highly complex forms.

Another recent advance is fully automated production, in which panels are produced using robotic arms in all aspects of fabrication, including cutting, nailing and installing insulation. This type of robotic fabrication contributes to reduced production costs and higher-quality products. Even though pre-fabrication has already made huge strides through innovation, there are plans to push the practice even further, from using products made from recycled materials to allowing customers to design and choose interior components online, according to space and budget.[12]

wall in that area, a key failure point in conventionally built walls: discontinuous insulation and an air barrier caused by improper installation. Tight, friction-fit joints and the ability to accommodate electrical boxes without interrupting the continuity of the insulation provides an attractive advantage over other construction methods. The relatively simple manufacturing techniques (with some not using adhesives) also provide continuous thermal breaks and adequate air barriers, making them likely to achieve consistent performance levels.

As is the case with any manufactured component, waste generation from pre-fabricated panel systems is less than would be expected from site construction. Assembling a wall system in a closed, controlled environment ensures that materials are used efficiently, and scrap pieces are more easily recovered and reused. The fact that the unit is closed within a short period of time also reduces delays caused by bad weather. Since there is less material wastage, the cost of clearing and removing debris is lowered.

Above left
**Roof and walls built
with SIPs.**

into the woods

Casa Algarrobo
Algarrobo, Chile
GA Estudio

Located near a coastal resort town in Chile, in a natural clearing surrounded by tall, dense trees, Casa Algarrobo is a creative example of a multi-generational home. The design had to accommodate the clients – three generations of one family, all with different personalities and needs, under one roof – and the challenge for the architects was to design a house that was flexible, as well as small in scale and within budget, using a series of identical modules to create individual spaces for everyone.

The cubic, single-storey home rests on a series of low concrete plinths, and looks like a combination of Ludwig Mies van der Rohe's modernist Farnsworth House and a cabin in the woods. Looking to the surrounding forest for inspiration, the architects formed a grid for the pre-fabricated modules, which was then repeated within the ordered volumes of the house to create a home that can be easily assembled or reassembled, like Lego bricks. The modules can be arranged into any number of configurations, and added to or removed, depending on the changing requirements of the family.

The design comprises two types of spaces: the public area, which opens onto the outdoor courtyard, and the private zones, with each enclosure separated from the others by introducing terraces and courtyards. In considering the circulation patterns generated by this spatial arrangement, the architects designed the shape of the building to mirror family relationships and movements: some are more distant, while others are closer, with a common centre that unites and guides them.

Below
Dining/living area.

Right
Site view.

The challenge for the architects was to design a multi-generational home that was flexible, as well as small in scale and within budget.

As a result, the house has an L-shaped floorplan, with five private bedrooms in one wing, and the shared living area, dining room and kitchen in the other. For privacy, each bedroom is separated from the others with an outdoor space; no two bedrooms share a wall, and all but one connect directly to a private deck. Adding to its modern appeal, the building is entirely panelled with wooden slats – laid horizontally on the exterior and vertically for the interiors. In contrast with the warm, natural tones of the timber used inside, most of the exterior walls have been stained in a dark grey. All of the modules feature large windows or fully glazed doors, allowing views of the private outdoor spaces without having to worry about the neighbours.

Casa Algarrobo delivers a logical, organized layout that functions as a multi-generational, pre-fabricated home for the whole family. Its small size was dictated by budget constraints, but the architects managed to deliver a spacious home that can be enjoyed by residents of all ages.

**Side view of the living
and dining areas.**

simple pleasures

Rubber House
Almere, Netherlands
Cityförster

**Side view
and entrance.**

The winning entry in the 2006 De Eenvoud ('simplicity') competition, Rubber House was chosen as one of twelve experimental housing projects to be built in Almere, next to a natural conservation area, on a site that is only accessible by a residential road (with the city centre and Ijmeer lake easily reached via a network of cycle paths). The focus on simplicity was not intended to be restrictive, but rather to promote a lifestyle that is not driven by material wealth.

Built with sustainable materials and energy-efficient, the single-family house takes its form from the archetypal Dutch barn. It features an asymmetrical, double-pitched roof over the two-storey section of the building, with a single-pitched roof over the single-storey portion. Inside, private spaces have been kept small to allow for a generous open-plan space, containing the kitchen, living area and pivoting fireplace, and expands out onto the terrace. The two-storey section has lower ceilings to accommodate multiple levels. On the ground floor is an office, bathroom and closet; the upper floor contains a bedroom with an en suite and walk-in closet.

The construction comprises massive wood panels made from cross-laminated timber, with the exterior clad in black EPDM foil, more commonly used on flat roofs. The dark, rough aesthetic of the material contrasts starkly with the cut-out forming the large terrace, itself clad in untreated larch, creating a transition to the inside. In contrast, the interior is characterized by the natural warmth of the wooden walls.

Above
Dining area.

Right
View of the living area.

Opposite
View of the terrace

The façade was designed using highly insulated and ventilated cavity construction. Following the concept of enabling self-build finishings, no conduit trenches were cut into the timber panels, with all MEP services and installations concentrated in a few plasterboard partitions and sockets recessed into the concrete floor. The house has underfloor heating, connected to the community heating network, with a wood stove providing additional warmth. Bathrooms are ventilated via controlled extract ductworks, and some of the windows are equipped with automatic opening vents.

The building is supported on a partly pre-fabricated ring foundation on top of twelve concrete piles. The ground-bearing slab is made from pre-cast, insulated hollow core slabs, with the load-bearing façades and the few load-bearing partitions built using cross-laminated timber panels. The roof was constructed from large, pre-fab insulated timber-frame panels, and was installed within a day. In fact, the amount of pre-fabrication in the project resulted in a construction period of three months for the entire home, with a significantly reduced amount of manual labour.

Rubber House demonstrates an innovative use of building materials, including the EPDM foil, which is not normally displayed on façades. It also utilizes sustainable materials and features energy-efficient products, as well as pre-fab components, which allow for ease and relative speed of construction.

cheap and cheerful

Happy Cheap House
Stockholm, Sweden
Tommy Carlsson Arkitektur

Resembling a cube with cut-off corners and clad in corrugated iron, Happy Cheap House is a prototype for an affordable, space-efficient update of the pre-fabricated homes commonly found throughout the Swedish suburbs. Architect Tommy Carlsson's design questions how much space people really need to live a comfortable life, and imagines what homes might look like in the future of compact housing trends.

By using a pre-fabricated modular frame of laminated plywood, the total cost of the project came to a mere €170,000 (£146,000, or $188,000). The frame's sandwich construction was chosen for its low-energy consumption in the factory, good installation value and excellent technical characteristics. The method also allows the shape of the building and the façade to be adapted to meet the client's requirements – in this case, the entire structure is clad in galvanized corrugated iron.

The design aims to optimize the internal space with a series of angled surfaces that define the interconnected ground-floor living areas and divide the upper storey into two bedrooms and a lounge. The house is located on a sloping site, with a series of shallow concrete steps that lead to an entrance sheltered beneath a corner sliced from the metal shell, creating a connection between the interior and the site. Much consideration went into designing the volume, and the close attention to detail continues in the façade and the outer geometry of the cube, which is clad in the same material to emphasize the volume as a whole.

The house is orientated with a large window facing southwest, with the façade giving the impression that the volume is inserted into the ground. The irregular roofline gives the building a sculptural appearance that changes when viewed from different angles, and reflects the unusual arrangement of the interior. Bent sheet-metal gutters jutting out from the two eaves funnel rainwater to the drainage channels below. Stained plywood was used to clad the internal surfaces of the porch to echo the interior, which is entirely constructed from plywood panels. The window openings are made from VFZ steel frames, with energy glass glued to them. Airing doors made from aluminium are a feature in the bedrooms, which have large fixed windows and ventilation hatches that can be closed during winter.

The ground level is generously recessed for the entrance, while the upper level opens up through a staircase, creating an open connection between the two levels. The kitchen has a large airing gap over the door and a shortcut to the garden. The staircase leads up to a common room, featuring two large windows. One is long and low, with a panoramic view to the southwest; the second window looks to the south. The two openings divide the living room into two natural spaces, creating an additional room when needed.

By employing pre-fabrication techniques, the architect has produced a design that achieves a compact home while reducing cost, without sacrificing either detailed features or comfort.

Right
**View to the ceiling
and upper floor.**

Opposite
Living and bedroom area.

Previous pages
Exterior view.

Above
Front elevation.

Right
View from the terrace.

la story

Living Homes Atwater
Los Angeles, California, USA
Living Homes

Atwater Village is one of the most desirable and vibrant neighbourhoods in Los Angeles, attracting the best of the city's boutiques, restaurants and cafés. As part of a new housing development, six factory-produced houses were built at the corner of Glendale Boulevard and La Clede Avenue, hoisted into place with the aid of a large crane. The architects collaborated with Rethink Development, one of the country's top design firms, to produce sustainable buildings in this luxury neighbourhood in the heart of Los Angeles.

The new community of three-bed, three-bath single-family homes is located in one of the most walkable areas in the city. The houses include private gardens with views of Los Angeles and the mountains from the upper floors and outdoor deck, as well as extensive windows, sliding doors and skylights, providing natural light and ventilation. The first floor contains the living room, kitchen and dining area in an open-plan arrangement. Most of the ground floor is dedicated to a garage for two cars.

The ground floor of each house was built on site in a conventional manner. The two upper floors, however, were fabricated in a factory in Oregon, and then shipped to site, allowing construction to be completed in three months, rather than twelve. Each module measures 16.2 × 4.9 × 3.4 m (53 × 16 × 11 ft), and arrived complete with everything from the wood siding and windows, to the plumbing, flooring, cabinets, countertops and lighting. After being put into place, the units only needed to be connected to the mains services.

The Living Homes designs feature Cradle to Cradle-certified wood floors and ceilings, formaldehyde-free millwork and siding, multiple sliding-glass doors, floor-to-ceiling glazing and clerestory windows, and light-tube and transom windows. Each home is solar-power ready and designed with ample storage. Atwater Village features an LEED Platinum-certified environmental programme, and to reduce energy, each house has energy-efficient lighting and appliances, and a smart HVAC system. Recycled materials were also used to reduce carbon emissions and waste. Low-flow water fixtures and a greywater-ready system help to minimize water consumption. Finally, the design used no VOC paints.

The project demonstrates many techniques and materials for designing and maintaining a sustainable home. In addition to providing green homes in which to live, Atwater Village also has plenty of amenities for leisure time, with the Los Angeles River and Griffith Park nearby.

Above
Bedroom.

Left
Dining room.

Opposite
Living area.

The effects of climate change and dwindling reserves of fossil fuels are forcing a widespread re-evaluation of traditional ways of harvesting and consuming energy. This in turn is heightening the need for new approaches to architectural design, with significant focus on sustainable buildings and building practices. Net-zero homes, which produce renewable energy greater or equal to the amount of their annual consumption, are one such venture into sustainable housing. These energy-efficient, pre-fabricated buildings generate their own power supply from on-site sources, enabling us to live in a more environmentally conscious way.

NET-ZERO HOMES

Approaches to net-zero buildings

A principal feature of net-zero homes is their independence from central power grids, with each building able to generate enough power on site for its own energy use. This type of sustainable design is considered 'active', and generally involves the use of solar and wind power, geothermal energy and a waste-water/heat-recovery system. A net-zero house can be off-grid (disconnected from the power-supply network and reliant on batteries for storing excess energy) or grid-tied, drawing from and feeding back into the local power grid, achieving a net-zero, or net-negative, sum of usage in accumulation.[13]

The use of renewable energy has been made widely possible by modern technologies. Such sources cannot be depleted through human use. The harvesting of power from the sun, the most abundant source of accessible energy, is achieved through advancements in photovoltaic cells, which convert solar energy into electricity.[14] Wind power can also be harvested through the conversion of kinetic energy into electricity through the use of specially designed wind turbines.[15] The choice of energy-production methods considers the context of a house design, and impacts the energy system. Considering that a large proportion of energy is often dedicated to heating the home, the energy system is commonly united with other heat-production methods, such as geothermal pumps and solar hot-water vacuum tubes.

'Passive' energy gain is the ability to conserve energy through minimizing unnecessary loss, and taking advantage of natural phenomena, rather than relying on mechanical systems to fulfil a function. A heavily context-orientated design is achieved by considering climate, topography, geology and ecology, and allows a building to be energy-efficient, using solar-energy gain, natural daylight and indoor airflow. The orientation and global positioning of a house also impact the design. A window that opens towards the sun, for example, is more energy-efficient than one that faces away from it: the same amount of heat is lost through the less-insulating window area, but solar-heat energy can counteract the effect.

The creation of a 'dynamic' envelope that integrates natural ventilation, passive solar gain and airtight insulation is critical to an energy-efficient, net-zero home, which must be well insulated to prevent air leakage. Common techniques that ensure a sealed envelope include the use of thick walls, wrap-and-strap, double-wall, truss-wall and cutting-edge thermal barrier materials.[16]

Pre-fabrication and net-zero homes

Manufacture in a controlled factory environment facilitates the introduction of new technologies, which in turn enable the active conservation of energy to be calculated, experimented with and implemented more easily. Designing an energy system to harvest and store enough energy for a household requires a rigorous research process beyond the realm of traditional construction techniques. Factory manufacture enables new technology and material innovations to be tested for cost-effectiveness prior to implementation, and provides flexibility for experimentation and making adjustments. Pre-fabrication also reduces the uncertainty of extraneous factors, such as weather and vandalism.[17] Its superior quality control allows for the build conditions necessary to achieve the energy-efficiency of a net-zero home, including the airtight sealing of doors and windows.

The precariousness of influencing factors in net-zero construction also makes factory-manufacturing more advantageous. To some extent, net-zero homes are individually customized for their context; traditional housing prototypes cannot be simply inserted and modified. Minor miscalculations – of the shadows created by neighbouring buildings, for example – can greatly hinder the proper functioning of a net-zero building.

Technologies range from sun, wind and heat capacity-calculating software to smart thermostats and energy-usage readers. Finally, pre-fabrication allows for mass-production in combination with mass-customization, increasing the affordability of net-zero homes.

An obstacle to the broad implementation of net-zero housing is early investment in customizing designs for each site, and the increased cost of the extra demand for insulation. The high investment costs can deter clients before they understand the later advantages. Mass-production and -customization of net-zero pre-fabricated homes inherently reduces manufacturing costs, and can also create net-zero communities that share a similar context, greatly reducing the cost for builders and creating a more affordable net-zero unit. Mass-production also allows manufacturers to create net-zero prototypes that help homebuyers understand the function of this relatively new concept.

Left
Camden Passivhaus, UK, Bere Architects.

material concerns

C3 Pre-fab
Chicago, Illinois, USA
Square Root

Chicago's high construction costs and strict building codes make it difficult to incorporate sustainable features into a home without sacrificing design or performance. Architect Jeffrey Sommers of Square Root began the design of C3 Pre-fab with the goal of balancing cost and energy-efficiency to provide a viable option for sustainable living. In the end, the solution was to pre-fabricate the house and make it semi-customizable. When complete, it became the first LEED Platinum-certified home in the city.

Although Sommers and his team used a pre-made foundation, the urban location and the 7.6 × 38 m (25 × 125 ft) lot with a 1 m (3 ft) setback to either side posed a construction challenge. The large modules had to make their way through the city and be assembled in the eight hours allowed for street closure. During construction, they were lifted 18 m (60 ft) in the air by crane to avoid hitting wires and trees. The pre-fab nature of the modules made it possible to build on the infill lot; normal construction methods would not have been able to meet the requirements necessary to build on such a narrow space.

Both the ground and first floors of the house have decks for expanded outdoor living, and a private courtyard between the living room and study lets in light and allows for natural ventilation. There is also a separate garage. Three types of materials were used for the cladding: reclaimed barn wood, fibre cement and corrugated Galvalume, which has a high recycled content and is low maintenance. On the ground floor, reclaimed engineered hickory flooring was used, with cork used for the first

floor for its affordability, warmth and sustainability. Other materials include recycled gypsum boards, non-VOC painted cabinetry with recycled content, and FSC-certified wood. The interior fittings, including the light fixtures and cabinetry, were chosen by the clients, and the colour palette also reflects their interests.

Sustainability initiatives include a water-catchment system and a living roof. Solar thermal panels collect heat, and are fitted with wires to allow for the addition of photovoltaic panels in the future. To increase energy-efficiency, the house has been supplied with a tankless water heater, energy-recovery ventilator, high-efficiency windows and a ductless mini-split system. LEDs (light-emitting diodes) and CFLs (compact fluorescent lamps) are used throughout the house, and the appliances are Energy Star-rated. Overall, the building achieves a blower-door test of 2.16 ACH at 50 pascals and a HERS rating of 48.

While there are many who would ideally choose the green-living option, in urban areas such as Chicago it is often beyond homeowners' means and is a difficult process to manage. Sommers and his team have produced a home that is affordable, functional, sustainable, desirable and, above all, appreciated by the clients.

Right
Rear yard.

Below
Living/dining areas.

Opposite
Living area.

passive control

Camden Passivhaus
London, UK
Bere Architects

The primary objective of this pioneering two-bedroom house – made from a heavily insulated pre-fabricated timber frame, set inside 3 m (10 ft) retaining walls and clad in European larch – was to create a comfortable home for the client and his young family, while minimizing energy consumption. The result, London's first Passivhaus, set benchmarks for energy-efficient design, thermal comfort and indoor-air quality.

Located on a challenging mews infill site, the house is cheap to run (achieving a heat saving of 90 per cent, compared to existing housing), is low in carbon emissions and is bright and airy, with sliding doors that look out onto a south-facing terrace. The term 'passivhaus' refers to an advanced low-energy construction standard for buildings with good ventilation and air-humidity levels year round, which are cool in summer and warm in winter with minimal heating, and free from draughts.

The urban site, and the shadows cast from adjacent buildings, had a major impact on the energy balance and design decisions. The Passive House Planning Package was used from the start of the project to determine the best position for the house and orientation of the glazing. The light-filled rooms have large, draught-free, triple-glazed windows to the south and west, while shade is provided by retractable external Venetian blinds with automatic solar control. In the summer, inward-tilting windows ensure night-time purge ventilation. Non-toxic materials and a heat-recovery ventilation system (which saves ten times the energy it uses) mean the air quality remains high.

Left
Cladding on the elevation.

Below
Detail of the façade.

Opposite
Living space.

Previous pages
Front elevation.

The primary objective of this pioneering house was to achieve a comfortable home for the client and his family, while minimizing energy consumption.

Mains water use is kept to a minimum by an underground rainwater-harvesting tank, which also provides water for the garden, a water-filtration system ensures that it is perfectly clean for drinking and bathing, and a solar thermal panel provides hot water via a tiny backup gas boiler. CO_2 emissions are reduced to 11.3 kg (25 lbs) per year, excluding appliances. Biodiversity was also important, so two wildflower-meadow roofs and an ivy-covered gabion stone wall were incorporated into the design.

affordable form

Krubiner Residence
Emeryville, California, USA
Swatt/Miers Architects

For this house in Emeryville, California, the goal was to take custom-quality modern architecture and produce an affordable product that could be packaged. The manufacturer, Simpatico Homes, followed a philosophy based on three core elements: form (modern), function (modular pre-fab) and footprint (green building). Together, they produced the Krubiner Residence, a prototype for modern, pre-fabricated sustainable houses.

Since its completion, Seth Krubiner, the founder of Simpatico Homes, has been living in the two-storey, single-family house. It was designed for a narrow infill lot – 30 × 9 m (100 × 30 ft) – in an established neighbourhood in the small city of Emeryville and comprises six modules with three bedrooms, three bathrooms, two outdoor terraces and a roof deck. The cost was much lower than other custom-built homes in the area, yet only required six months to construct.

The house is LEED-certified with 6.2-kilowatt solar panels, allowing Krubiner to sell the excess energy produced back to the grid. The thirty-panel photovoltaic solar system on the roof takes advantage of California's annual average of 260 days of sunshine. There is also an expansive roof deck and a living green roof, which increases insulation, absorbs rainwater and reduces run-off. The rooftop garden is tiled with Tray Green, made from 100 per cent recycled materials, with built-in handles to allow access to the roof structure. The trays are planted with succulents, which can withstand the hot sun and dry conditions.

was used, which is not only aesthetic, but is also durable and has a long lifespan. Insulated concrete blocks were used in the walls of the garage and in the living room. Because they do not require exterior cladding or interior drywall, the blocks are cost-effective. They work best for walls that do not require plumbing, and allow the house to be built on a slab foundation. In Emeryville's hot, dry climate, a well-insulated house reduces the amount of energy needed for air-conditioning.

This Simpatico Homes prototype responds and adapts to the geographic and situational conditions of its location to achieve a net-zero house. It demonstrates sustainability, attractiveness, affordability and practicality, all of which are essential in promoting pre-fabricated homes to a broader audience.

California's average annual rainfall of 584 mm (23 in.) can result in severe drought conditions, so rainwater catchment for irrigation is extremely important. Modular rainwater storage tanks (or HOGs) were chosen for their space-efficiency, owing to their slim form and ability to fit beneath downspouts without interfering with the walkway. The house has two 189- litre (50-gallon) tanks that link together, allowing the possibility for expansion.

An electric heat pump and hydronic radiant sub-floor heating ensure energy-efficiency, and the fixtures and appliances were also chosen for their performance capabilities. Passive solar design was considered when planning the house, which has floor- to-ceiling Energy Star windows. To protect the exterior wall, engineered-wood rainscreen cladding

The manufacturer followed a philosophy based on three core elements: form, function and footprint.

Above
Living room.

Left
Kitchen/dining area.

Opposite
Hallway.

Previous pages
Exterior view.

here comes the sun

57th & Vivian – Solar Laneway House
Vancouver, British Columbia, Canada
Lanefab Design/Build

A 'laneway' house is a small-scale, detached building, typically built in the garden of a pre-existing single-family home, which opens onto the back lane. Although laneway houses have been present in Canada for many years, owing to the increase in urban density and property costs, they are gaining popularity in the greater Vancouver area. Local company Lanefab Design/Build constructed the city's first net-zero, solar laneway house at 95 m² (1,023 sq ft) – the maximum allowed – comprising one bedroom, one-and-a-half baths and a garage.

As a solution to unnecessary energy consumption, the house was built using SIPs (pre-fabricated structural insulated panels), which are strong, energy-efficient and cost-effective, and R40 insulation in the walls, 30 cm (1 ft)-thick. Common to homes across Vancouver, the exterior features blackrock stucco and cedar cladding. Windows were positioned on the south-facing façade to take advantage of natural heat and light, and triple-glazed Cascadia windows and doors were installed to prevent heat loss. Multi-fold doors extend the living/dining area into the outdoor space during the warmer months, where the southern orientation offers passive solar heating.

Twelve solar panels were placed on the roof to generate extra power when the weather is dry and sunny, which is then sold to the grid. During the winter months, with their overcast skies and long periods of rain, the building draws on the surplus of power stored over the summer. This photovoltaic system allows the house to have as much energy as it needs throughout the year.

An air-source heat pump provides space-heating and hot water to control the heat transfer between inside and out. Additionally, 95 per cent of the lighting used in the house comes from LEDs, which are more efficient and have a longer lifespan than traditional incandescent lightbulbs. The house's overall energy consumption is measured by a Cent-a-Meter energy monitor.

On average, Vancouver has 168 rainy days and over 140 cm (55 in.) of precipitation per year. To take advantage of these wet conditions, the house includes an in-ground tank for harvesting rainwater. A drain-water heat-recovery system preheats cold water entering the water heater by collecting heat from warm greywater, and a Venmar high-efficiency heat-recovery ventilator provides air circulation and energy-efficient heating. One of the benefits of the heat-recovery ventilator is that it substantially reduces the amount of energy required to heat or cool the home, because ventilation occurs without having to open the window, thus preventing loss of heat.

Vancouver's high-priced housing market provides a challenge for those who want to own their own home in such a densely urban area. The low construction cost of Lanefab's net-zero laneway house, however, makes this dream affordable, as well as allowing for economic and environmentally sustainable methods of development.

Above
Front and side elevations.

Right
Kitchen/living area.

One of the challenges facing the contemporary housing market is the sheer range of potential clients, with traditional layouts no longer suitable to their ever-shifting requirements. The vast spectrum of homebuyers' wishes has led to the need for increased customization. This, in turn, means that current practices in home design and construction must also change. One solution is mass-customized communities, in which entire developments are designed to offer a better fit between residents and their homes using pre-fabricated methods.

INNOVATIVE COMMUNITIES

Motives for mass-customized communities

A sustainable housing market is one that considers the socio-economic concerns of residents, as well as environmental challenges. The emergence of non-traditional families, together with the limited financial resources and non-standard demands of some homebuyers, has changed contemporary housing. The convenience of online shopping and exposure to a wide range of lifestyles has also led to a new approach in determining home desirability: customization. The need to suit each home to a buyer makes the search for customized design and production highly relevant.[18]

Mass-customization requires coordination between the architect, manufacturer, builder and consumer. The development of generative models for integrating buyers' needs in the early stages of a design has been promising, but the process raises questions concerning its efficiency and applicability. Implementing a design for mass-customization depends mainly on the chosen business model. In other words, the housing typology, production technology and marketing strategy all dictate the level of customer intervention in the design process.

'Quality' and 'affordability' are often-used terms in the housing market, yet they can be at odds when budget-driven conventional technologies are implemented. Industrialization holds the key to lowering the cost of standardized building components through a streamlined process that is both time- and material-efficient, with reduced labour demands.[19] Mass-production makes homes that are both affordable and of good quality possible, but the process is inevitably connected with the monotony of repetitive units, and at odds with the demand for design customization. A solution to the challenge of maximizing new technologies while satisfying rising demands is mass-customization, which can be applied at both the unit and community scales.

Forms of mass-customization

Different manufacturers have different ways of offering customization to homebuyers. One of the easiest and most popular is to integrate standard products and services.[20] In other words, prior to delivery, customers choose standardized products from a catalogue to be customized during the marketing stage.[21] This method can include offering varieties of single-storey homes, townhouses and single-family residences as part of one integrated community. It involves the least need for radical changes in the manufacturer's value chain, and is the most easily adaptable to the conventional housing industry.

Some pre-fabrication companies, including Living Homes (see p. 26) and Postgreen Homes, have developed interactive, web-based platforms that engage customers in the design by taking them through a series of decision-making processes. Clients begin by choosing a housing model, and then proceeding with modifications, with a support system providing details of finishing materials.

Left
**Floating Houses IJburg,
Netherlands, Marlies
Rohmer.**

Any change to the base unit is reflected in the price. At the end of the process, the customer gets a detailed analysis and the final cost. The manufacturers themselves usually depend on standardization of components, with different assembly options.

A second approach, which better exploits the advantages of standardization, is the mass-production of customizable end products. This method is adaptable to clients' requirements, and is especially useful when those needs change over time. With this system, designs can be customized, even after purchase, through the selection of alternative end products, and mass-produced to work with a universal plug-in system. It is important to note that a system for customized housing requires the input of a homebuyer's socio-cultural background, building context, budget and desired spaces and activities, all of which are accommodated into a set of precise spatial requirements that will structure the design brief.

Planning mass-customized communities

Despite the common misbelief that mass-production techniques at a community design scale produce monolithic, repetitive units, they can achieve the opposite when combined with mass-customization and a holistic design. The overall site planning, design and location of all buildings, homes, car parks, public gardens, play areas, and connections to other neighbourhoods and amenities are often overseen by one architectural company, which will work with engineers and other contractors to incorporate contemporary technologies and sustainable features. Many such sites feature shared spaces and car-free circulation to enhance a greater sense of community.[22]

In recent years, mass-customized developments have emerged as an alternative to conventional subdivisions. In addition to the economic advantages they offer, such mass-customized communities can be more sustainable, while also satisfying a wider range of residents' needs.

a room of one's own

Y: Cube Mitcham
London, UK
Rogers Stirk Harbour & Partners

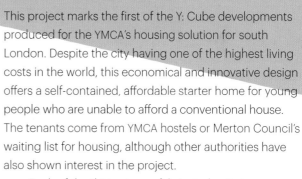

This project marks the first of the Y: Cube developments produced for the YMCA's housing solution for south London. Despite the city having one of the highest living costs in the world, this economical and innovative design offers a self-contained, affordable starter home for young people who are unable to afford a conventional house. The tenants come from YMCA hostels or Merton Council's waiting list for housing, although other authorities have also shown interest in the project.

Each of the thirty-six pre-fabricated units is a one-bedroom studio for single occupancy, with a variety of exterior colours and designs. The units are built in a factory in Derbyshire, before being transported to London. They arrive on site with all of the services included, so the utilities – water, heating and electrics – can be easily connected. One unit takes a week to build in the factory, with each costing between £30,000 and £35,000 ($39,000 and $45,500). Although the manufacturing costs are high, the costs of management are significantly reduced on site, when the blocks are put into place.

The modular construction means that additional units can be added or removed, and the entire development, with a total area of 1,640 m² (17,650 sq ft), disassembled and relocated up to five times during its sixty-year lifespan. There is no waste on site, and disruptions and construction noise are kept to a minimum. The units themselves are made from high-quality, ecologically sensitive materials, such as renewable timber, and achieve Level 6 in the UK Code for Sustainable Homes.

The units are made from high-quality, ecologically sensitive materials, and achieve Level 6 in the UK Code for Sustainable Homes.

The timber frame is lined with medium-density fibreboard and simple cement rainscreen cladding. In the factory, the pods have a tolerance of 2 mm (0.07 in.), meaning that they are well insulated and require little or no heating, even in winter. The small amount of energy required to heat the home keeps costs down, with gas and electricity bills as low as £10 ($13) per month.

The width of the rooms and pitch of the shallow roofs vary, as the dimensions are determined by the maximum cargo-width of the lorry used for transportation. Each apartment has a living space with a galley kitchen, as well as its own front door, allowing each resident his or her own sense of place. The units are also designed to provide good acoustics and natural lighting. Outside, wide timber decks provide additional living space, overlooking a grassy courtyard.

The YMCA allows tenants to live in the apartments for up to five years. During that time, residents can save for a deposit, aided by the affordable rent and low utility bills. Y: Cube is a better alternative for those of limited means than poor-quality shared accommodation, providing a solution to housing needs within the community, as well as giving tenants opportunities for independence.

Courtside elevation.

community care

Floating Houses IJburg
Amsterdam, Netherlands
Marlies Rohmer

The Dutch have a history of living close to the water, and coping with the challenges that come with it. Houseboats and floating hotels or restaurants are no strangers to the canals of the Netherlands. Recently, however, with two-thirds of the population already living below sea level, a perception has been growing that there is a shortage of land, accompanied by a renewed enthusiasm for living on the water. Architect Marlies Rohmer's project, with seventy-five units and a total area of 10,652 m² (114,657 sq ft), embraces this idea and removes further pressures on housing in the country's metropolitan areas.

This floating neighbourhood is close to amenities, including schools and restaurants, and a tram that takes residents into the centre of Amsterdam in fifteen minutes. During the summer, they can swim in the lake surrounding their homes, or skate on its frozen surface in winter. The buildings themselves are more similar to land-based houses than to boats, and are classified as immovable properties. Together, they represent a community, laid out in a triangular shape dictated by the diagonal slicing of the basin by the power lines. To provide space for boats, a sense of individuality and a continually changing view, the houses vary in orientation and proximity to other units.

Although living on the water is not a new concept, it is a very different proposition to building on land. The houses are built in a shipyard about 65 km (40 miles) north of the IJ lake and transported along canals, restricting the width of the houses to 6.5 m (21 ft) or less. Each one is supported by a buoyant concrete tub, which is submerged

Right
Hauling a unit to site.

Below
Living area.

Previous pages
Summer scene.

With two-thirds of the population already living below sea level, there has been a renewed enthusiasm for living on the water.

to the depth of half of a storey. Above, a lightweight steel construction is fitted with wooden panelling to create rooms and floors. This steel frame can be covered with brightly coloured panelling, which can be altered later by residents according to taste or the need for privacy. Finally, to prevent the houses from floating away or into one another, they are anchored to the lake bed by steel mooring plates.

Across the units, the partly submerged lowest storey generally contains the bathrooms and bedrooms. The kitchen and dining area, with a covered veranda, is on the raised ground floor, with the main living area on the top floor, connected to a cantilevered open-terrace deck. Despite their similar appearance, there are multiple layouts possible for each unit, including pre-designed extension packages that offer further customization – for sun rooms, verandas, awnings, and more, which can be easily attached to the skeleton frame. Owing to the height difference on the ground floor between the jetty, the water and the front door, these elements are bridged by a boardwalk that circles around the house and slopes down to the water.

This project is an experiment in living on water without the feeling of being on a boat. Floating homes provide housing in a dense urban area, and eliminate the constant worry that comes with living on land so close to the water. Unlike the flood-prevention structures that inhibit growth, this floating community allows for the redevelopment of obsolete dock areas or flooded quarries, and an expansion into a new arena for urban development.

Above
Pre-fab unit.

new in town

Town House
Manchester, UK
ShedKM

Town House is a new housing project in Manchester, comprising thirty-six row houses. The scheme is an experiment with adaptable, mass-produced homes to address the UK's housing shortage, and a modern twist on the traditional terraced house, allowing for both customization and flexible layouts. Clients can choose the layout of their homes from a surprising number of options, despite the similar façades. The project also offers them the chance to remain in the city centre, rather than moving out to the suburbs.

Houses are delivered to site as raw shells, with kitchens and bathrooms already in place. After the timber-framed pods are lifted into position, partition walls are added according to the specified layout. The modular construction allows each unit to be completed in two to three weeks, without disrupting the neighbourhood, while off-site production ensures that standards and tolerances have been monitored in a controlled environment, reducing waste and producing energy-efficient homes.

Although the placement of the kitchens and bathrooms are fixed, residents can decide if they want a loft- or garden-living arrangement. Layouts are tailored for one- to five-bedroom homes, with an open or traditional floorplan. The houses have two or three storeys, with the traditional option of having the living space at the lower level, or taking the 'upside-down' route, with the communal areas on the upper levels of the house. Balconies, parking spaces and private gardens are also available as additions to the homes.

Each house has the same exterior grey panelling, roofing and articulated windows. All units have a long, narrow form, with a slender, pitched roof running the length of the building. The metal cladding of the roof not only visually separates it from the brick elevation, but also allows the units to be distinguishable at street level from neighbouring houses, as do the extruding black-framed windows at both ends, which create a bay window in the living area and master bedroom, allowing more light to penetrate into the home.

The Town House concept offers mass-produced structures that are energy-efficient and cheaper than city-centre flats, and are flexible enough to meet the needs of the various residents. It has been adapted for use in other areas of the UK. As a result of this initial project, architects ShedKM, together with regeneration company Urban Splash, have set a precedent to help further reduce costs and construction time for future developments.

Left
Kitchen.

Previous pages
Front view.

The scheme is an experiment with adaptable, mass-produced homes to address the UK's housing shortage.

Left
Canal side of townhouses.

Above
Living area.

room to grow

Grow Community
Bainbridge Island, Washington, USA
Davis Studio

Grow Community, the first phase of a multi-generational development, is already the largest solar community in the state of Washington. The twenty-three single-family homes and twenty multi-family units (available in four models: 'Aria', 'Ocean', 'Tallis' and 'Everett') form a net-zero community, just five minutes' walk from the amenities of downtown Winslow and a thirty-five-minute ferry ride from Seattle. The project has been endorsed as a One Planet Living community, which promotes a happy and healthy lifestyle, while using fewer of the earth's resources.

Grow Community is net-zero and zero-carbon, with net-positive homes and community gardens. About 60 per cent of the neighbourhood is dedicated to peaceful, natural spaces, with shared gardens to help feed residents. Surplus crops are donated to a local food bank. There are parks and playgrounds, with walkways throughout for easy pedestrian access. Along with parking for residents, there is a free electric car- and bike-sharing programme, over 6,000 m² (64,500 sq ft) of open space and bioswales that clean the water before it flows into Puget Sound.

To encourage sustainability and higher density, the development has been built under a zoning ordinance approved by the city of Bainbridge Island. As a result, the footprint of each building is small; houses range from 107 to 171 m² (1,155 to 1,846 sq ft) and two-bedroom apartments from 84 to 98 m² (900 to 1,050 sq ft). Studio apartments are 42 m² (450 sq ft). As the development welcomes people of all ages, there are homes for single-level living with lift access to front entrances.

Grow Community, the first phase of a multi-generational development, is already the largest solar community in the state of Washington.

Above
Exterior view of several homes.

Opposite
Living room.

Previous pages
Wood-clad solar-powered houses.

All single-family homes and duplexes have photovoltaic panels, and future developments will have the option to add them. Choosing the solar-power option is beneficial not only for the environment, but also for residents, as there are financial incentives. Owners of homes that incorporate locally made solar equipment receive a stipend each year to help power the rooftop generators. It is estimated that the addition of photovoltaic panels will have a full return on investment within five years, while also lowering energy bills and creating more sustainable homes.

Walls and roofs are built in a factory, which allow the houses to be constructed in five to six months, with minimal waste. The materials used during the build are, when possible, locally sourced and renewable. The houses are also airtight, with R38 blown-in fibreglass insulation in the walls and R60 in the attics. As a result, the insulation exceeds the state energy code by at least 30 per cent. LED lighting, low-flow fixtures and energy-efficient appliances have also been used, as have double-paned windows that let in natural light, highly efficient heat pumps and heat-recovery ventilators.

When Grow Community is completed, there will be fifty houses, eighty-one multi-family units and a community centre. Unlike the LEED programme, One Planet Living focuses not only on green buildings, but also on creating whole neighbourhoods. The architects have managed to design a community that is as green as possible, while keeping the houses and apartments affordable.

The highly innovative Japanese pre-fab housing industry has developed a user-orientated approach by integrating specially developed marketing, design and quality-orientated techniques into its production processes. Customization is delivered through holistic management and balancing the use of standard components with flexibility of assembly. With manufacturers continually striving to bridge the communication gap between themselves and their clients to offer successful mass-customized designs, homebuyers benefit from a sense of ownership and individuality. In turn, the manufacturers benefit from customer satisfaction and a positive reputation in the market.

JAPANESE HOMES

Pre-fab housing in Japan

Japan's prefabricated-housing industry is a world leader in innovation, with efficient production processes, targeted marketing strategies and consumer outreach, and high-quality designs that offer variability and flexibility at affordable prices. A fully computerized system enables clients to customize their homes with standardized components. Unlike the common Western perception about pre-fabrication, in Japan factory-manufactured houses are seen as superior to conventionally built ones.[23]

In the post-war period, Japan began experimenting with pre-fab housing to meet demand, and factory manufacturing became more popular. One of the reasons behind this trend was that houses have a short lifespan in Japan – an average of twenty-six years – and homebuyers often prefer to build their own.[24] The country's population is roughly twice that of the UK, yet over six times as much new housing is built in Japan than in the UK each year. A family that outgrows its home will simply tear it down and build a new one on the same site, and some companies now offer deals for house replacement: a maximum fifty-day period (including weekends) from moving out to moving in. This style of construction makes a fully customizable production process particularly advantageous.

The urgent demand for housing in the 1960s and '70s also provided an opportunity, as conventional home construction was unable to saturate the housing market owing to a shortage of materials and labour. As a result, manufactured homes provided an affordable alternative, drastically accelerating their wider acceptance.[25]

Marketing strategies and consumer outreach

A main feature of Japanese pre-fab housing is the extensive system for mass-customization, with a high level of consumer participation throughout the process. A modular production method is used, with manufacturers focusing on a custom design for each unit, while mass-producing a variety of housing components for clients to choose from. This system is critical to satisfying the array of demands of the diverse homebuyer demography and to controlling costs through mass-production and economy of scale.

The industry achieved its reputation through an attention to quality control. Manufacturers take pride in knowing that once their homes leave the highly rationalized assembly-line setting, few consumers can distinguish a factory-made home from a traditional 'stick-built' one, in either Japanese or Western styles.[26] Public education through information centres play a key role in advertising these homes, offering technical information about materials, construction methods and amenities. They also function as exhibition and consultation bases, where staff advise clients on customization, from external appearance to floorplans, with the aid of advanced computer technology.

Left
**A-Ring, Japan,
Atelier Tekuto.**

Design features

In Japan, pre-fab homes are mass-customized using primarily a standardized component system for structural, exterior and interior arrangements. To provide the necessary flexibility, a modular system is employed, in which housing components are divided into the categories of volume, exterior and interior, and fitted in a variety of ways using a universal connector system. The volume components are used in building the structure that determines the number and size of each type of room, while the interior and exterior components serve to coordinate the decorative and the functional elements that customize a home.[27]

The concept of volume components often applies to modular pre-fabricated homes, because a panellized housing system does not define spatial limitations for a volume of interior space. In the design process of panellized homes, however, a modular logic is similarly applied, based on the size of the traditional *tatami* mat

(90 × 180 cm, or 3 × 6 ft), which forms the basic unit of a room and provides a convenient measure against which manufacturers can produce unit components. Each structural unit is then treated as a box-shaped frame component, with spatial variations defined by a combination of these standard units.

Exterior components that define the visual identity of a house from the outside – roof, walls, windows, verandas, balconies and entrances – are vital in fostering a sense of ownership, with the client participating in the design. Catalogues, design-consultancy services and information centres that offer real samples of built constructions are available to aid clients with their decisions and to put them at ease.

house of the spirits

House of 33 Years
Nara, Japan
Assistant

Designed by architectural firm Assistant and located next to the Todaiji Temple in Nara, this home was built for an elderly couple who decided to move after thirty-three years in their previous home. The house was built in three different cities, and represents a collection of memories and the future, both existing simultaneously in a single space. By using a variety of materials to create frames in the façade and the interior, images are continuously produced by the movements of the residents.

The fabrication of the house was supported by the Aomori Contemporary Art Centre and Sendai School of Design, and comprises several pavilions and timber rooms beneath an exterior skin. The relationship between the individual elements defines the character of the building as a whole. The exterior steel roof was constructed on site, while the other components of the house were divided into two programmes, one for each participating institution, with the Sendai School of Design building a pavilion to be used as the first floor.

A structure entitled 'Ghost House' was built with students from the local university to sit on the roof of the building. The main rooms were constructed in Aomori by local carpenters, using native timber, and were used for an installation piece – *Obscure Architecture* – as part of the *Kime to Kehai: Texture and Sense* exhibition at the Aomori Contemporary Art Centre. Once the exhibition was over, the elements were disassembled and transported to Nara on a lorry, where the house was rebuilt under one roof to become a single entity.

A pitched roof covers the series of timber-framed pavilions and rooms of various sizes, layered one on top of each other. The social areas – living, dining and kitchen – are located in an open space at the back of the house. At the front, next to the entrance, are the bathroom and bedroom. Steel staircases access the upper level and terraces. The exterior walls, which were built on site, use a range of materials, including brick, corrugated polycarbonate, galvanized steel, expanded metal and steel mesh, while the glass panels and sliding wood doors allow visual connections between the interiors, creating varying levels of transparency, through which silhouettes of movement can be seen.

The House of 33 Years was built after much consideration of the clients' merging of their past and their future. The couple brought their memories and belongings from the past, but recognized their new home as a place where fresh experiences would be formed. The house also contains the memories of the people who were involved in its construction, with the process demonstrating that not all pre-fabricated homes come from factories.

Left
Kitchen.

Below
Side view at night.

Opposite left
View into living area.

Opposite right
Hallway.

a is for aluminium

A-Ring
Ishikawa, Japan
Atelier Tekuto

This pre-fab home follows on from the previous two models in Atelier Tekuto's Aluminium Project. In collaboration with a number of universities and companies, the architects explored materials and technologies for use in a design that can exist symbiotically with the environment, with the aim of the exercise being to develop a single piece of aluminium that could serve various functions at once. In 2008, one year before it was completed, A-Ring received an inaugural grant as part of Japan's efforts to reduce carbon-dioxide emissions caused by the construction industry.

The main structure incorporates an aluminium ring and column and beam frame. Four aluminium moulds, developed by the architects and their partners, interlock to form the ring. The modified deck plate moulds, comprising columns, walls and binding joists, are held together using a single basic dice mould and ordinary bolts. As a result, the team was able to reuse materials, reduce waste and achieve a higher construction quality. Composite units combining structure, a heating/cooling system and water section were also developed. The ring integrates the radiant heating/cooling system into the house by passing a pipe through the pre-fabricated aluminium components, creating a large radiator and further structural elements. 'Wet' functions such as bathroom and kitchen units were built into the aluminium rings.

To minimize running costs and the environmental footprint, the house relies on natural-energy systems. An energy-harnessing unit is embedded into the ring.

Left
**View from bathroom
to living area.**

Opposite, above and below
Living space.

Previous pages
Front and top views.

The system was developed to obtain heat from groundwater and geothermal energy through solar power, reducing energy costs by half. LED lights are incorporated into the structure, which makes use of aluminium's reflective properties to illuminate a greater area. All other light fixtures were replaced with LEDs, reducing energy consumption by 80 per cent. 'Green curtains' reuse captured rainwater and a 'passive fence' is formed by sprinkling water inside the frame. A roof garden on the second floor helps with the collection of rainwater. By passing a hemp cord through an aluminium frame, the plants wrap around the cord to create a natural curtain. Rainwater tanks were installed to allow water to circulate inside the frame, with some of it used to mist the plants and cool the inside of the house.

In the months after the completion of the house, experiments were conducted to measure the effectiveness of its innovative systems. Following initial assessments, someone will move in to continue monitoring the results. The various units developed in the construction of A-Ring will enhance energy- and material-efficiency, with the building itself testing the systems in readiness for the market. The use of aluminium is still relatively rare in the building industry, and data gathered from this project may help it become an essential building material, alongside concrete, steel and wood.

national grid

Module Grid House
Saitama, Japan
Tetsuo Yamaji Architects

Pre-fabricated homes have been around in Japan for decades, and many people are in favour of the idea of a mass-produced home. When pressed, however, most said that they would not buy one. Everyone, it seems, wants a house that is unique to their needs and situation, while at the same time being like everyone else. Module Grid House in Saitama is a non-mass-produced home for young families, made from pre-fabricated components, using a construction method that provides a high-quality building for a low cost.

Shakkanho is the traditional measurement system in Japan, used before the adoption of the metric system. In the construction industry, it is still the preferred method, especially for wood construction, as using a modular system with standardized components ensures cost-efficiency. Module Grid House is based on grids of *tatami* mats, with each grid measuring 9 × 9 m (30 × 30 ft); the floor area is six grids by eight, with a height of four grids.

The two-storey, flat-roofed home has an exposed timber frame, with the private spaces – bedroom and bathroom – located on the ground floor. The floor above contains a large open living space with a dining area and kitchen. A gridded window on the east wall spans the entire living room, supported by wooden beams, with a door integrated into it. The window opens onto a terrace, which sits above the entrance canopy, for outdoor dining. The expanse of glazing provides an abundance of natural light, complementing the warm atmosphere created by the low hanging lights in the kitchen.

The exposed wooden frame can best be seen on the exterior of the building, forming the eaves. Rafters on the first-floor ceiling are mass-produced, 6 m (20 ft) in length with a width of 1.2 × 1.2 m (4 × 4 ft). Using timber with specific measurements, there is no waste, because the excess is incorporated into the eaves. Other elements of the house are also dependent on mass-produced components to be both cost-efficient and reduce waste. The exterior is clad in corrugated metal, while the interior is painted white. To echo the timber framing, the kitchen is made from plywood. Wooden floors are also available as an alternative to *tatami* mats.

Although the architects make use of the *shakkanho* system of measurement and other traditional components, they have been altered to create a different order. Using this method of construction offers the benefits of pre-fabrication, while allowing for customization to meet the needs of the residents. This home is not only cost-efficient, therefore, but challenges common misconceptions about pre-fabricated homes and components.

Right
Stairway.

Below
Wood-frame construction detail.

Opposite
Kitchen and large window.

The need to reduce urban sprawl and to increase density, along with a desire to reside in the heart of the city, has increased the appeal of infill homes for planners, builders and homebuyers alike. Building a house with a width of less than 5 m (16 ft) on a similarly narrow lot makes pre-fabrication a rapid and efficient method of construction. This type of housing has the potential to improve the urban fabric, and to increase density in a dispersed manner, without changing the appearance of the neighbourhood. High-density infill homes also allow residents to participate in the rehabilitation of their own communities.[28]

NARROW DESIGNS

Advantages of infill units

Infill houses are beneficial economically, owing to the infusion of additional tax revenues, with the compact design adding further advantages: joining units of row houses reduces both the square footage of lots and lengths of streets, saving on land costs, as well as energy consumption, as heat loss is limited to fewer exterior walls and a smaller roof area.

Merging four detached homes into two semi-detached houses reduces the exposed wall area by 36 per cent, and into a four-unit terrace by another 50 per cent. Heat-loss reduction of approximately 21 per cent can be achieved when two dwellings are attached, and a further 36 per cent savings for the middle unit or units when three or more units are joined.[29] Grouping houses is also an effective means of improving efficiency during construction. The repetition of parts usually results in a shorter build time per house, and a reduction in perimeter area can also have a significant impact on delivery time, as the construction of the envelope is labour-intensive and costly.

Designing efficient interiors

Various approaches to the interior design of narrow homes have been suggested over the years, the outcome of cultural attitudes, trends and, of course, whether the building is attached or detached. Designers of traditional houses have tended to enclose and separate the various functions from one another. The dining room, for example, was formal, with its own proportions and doorway. In the 20th century, this organization was relaxed and replaced by the open plan, which saw rooms flow into one another with no partitions.[30] Living, dining and kitchen spaces were merged into a single, large area. The sleeping zone, on the other hand, retained its traditional format, with each bedroom enclosed – although a loft-type design can be found in which an entire level, with the exception of the plumbing fixtures, is left open.

When homes are built in a row, exposure to natural light becomes critical. Ideally, each function has some exposure to daylight, but as this is often not possible, it becomes necessary to prioritize. The tendency is to locate the kitchen and living room at a house's extremes, with the bedrooms at either end on the upper floor. On both levels, the centre is occupied by utility and service functions, for which the penetration of natural light is less important.[31] Careful attention must be paid to movement through the floors and the location of the stairs. In general, the aim is to reduce the amount of space allocated to circulation. The architect is likely to try to assign most of the area to the functions themselves. The common approach would be to use the less-lit areas for movement; in townhouses, this is the axis along the longitudinal wall.

Despite the narrow width, there are a number of possibilities for locating a stair and designing circulation in an infill house. Different staircase types may occasionally

Pre-fabrication of narrow homes

Construction practices have evolved in recent years, and continue to do so. Innovation has brought new building products to the fore that reduce the use of natural resources and save money for builders and consumers. Some of these have gained acceptance and are widely used, while others have encountered resistance. Two of the main products are engineered timber and light-gauge steel, both of which are used for joists, beams and flooring. Glue-laminated (glulam) boards are made from stacked, finger-jointed layers of standard timber.

Heat loss through the building envelope occurs as a result of conduction, convection or radiation. In all three cases, windows are the weakest link in the envelope's thermal performance, and therefore are the most important investment in the construction or renovation of any building. They vary enormously in price, appearance and performance, making choosing them a difficult process.

Narrow homes lend themselves to pre-fab techniques, because the reduced dimensions are suitable for factory production and transportation. These buildings are also often present in masterplanned neighbourhoods, which tend to be subject to mass-production and -customization.

be combined to respond to the layouts of various floors. Stairs are typically located at either the front or middle of an entrance level, and it is practical to place them near the entrance for fast and easy access to the upper levels. Locating them at the rear of the house is less desirable, as they would be further from the entrance and would block natural light. The location and chosen type determines the layouts of the upper and lower levels. Arriving at the middle of the sleeping floor or attic is preferable, as this would free the extreme ends for bedrooms. This is less of a priority in a basement, as the arrangement of functions is less formal.

Above left
**Pre-fab infill home in
Brussels, Belgium.**

boogie down

Bronx Box
New York, New York, USA
Resolution: 4 Architecture

After twenty years of living in a small bungalow at the foot of Throgs Neck Bridge in the New York City borough of the Bronx, the Marengo family decided they needed a bigger house, but were not willing to sacrifice the waterfront location. Because of the narrow lot, the width of the existing house could not be increased, and the foundations could not support an additional level. As a result, Mrs Marengo, herself a structural engineer, suggested a pre-fab building that could be built quickly with minimal disruption to the area.

Bronx Box, at 4.9 m (16 ft) wide, comprises two modules, which when joined together form a volume that is twice the size of the previous home. Restrictions in the zoning envelope, setbacks, height and floorplan have resulted in a compact footprint, complete with off-street parking, a small green space and an expansive roof deck. The design is part of the single-bar series, a modified version of the double-decker, two-storey bar typology, with an additional storage 'saddlebag' and built-in cabinets.

On the ground floor, a wall of built-in storage runs the entire length of the building, and an open living, dining and kitchen area opens out onto an elevated deck. Exterior stairs at the back stretch across the full width of the house and lead down to a pier that protrudes into Eastchester Bay. The first floor imitates the linear organization of the floor below; the top floor has two bedrooms and two-and-a-half baths, one of which is an en suite. The master bedroom has its own fireplace and balcony, with a skylight in the bathroom.

Above
Living room and deck.

Opposite
Front façade.

Materials used for the interiors include maple for the cabinets, bamboo for the floors, slate in the bathrooms and Caesarstone for the countertops. Outside, cement boards were used for cladding with cedar accents. The roof was made from Galvalume, a coating that comprises zinc, aluminium and silicon, and the deck from ipe wood, owing to its low maintenance requirements. The roof bulkhead, which was designed carefully to be within zoning restrictions, gives access to an expansive roof deck, with a 360° view of the water and surrounding neighbourhood. This modern home also makes use of the colours and textures found in the urban fabric by incorporating them into the design.

Pre-fabricated houses are restricted to the 5 m (16 ft) width of the lorry transporting them to site, and can only be widened minimally through the use of 'saddlebags', which cantilever slightly to provide enough space for storage. They have the potential to be more cost-effective, the Bronx Box cost just over £400,000 (or just over $500,000), much less than buying a new house in the area or using conventional building methods. But there are other, greater benefits to having a pre-fabricated home, including sustainability and time-efficiency.

small packages

Smallhouse
Switzerland
Bauart Architekten

What would constitute an ideal house? A large space, perhaps, one in which to eat, sleep and work? Smallhouse by Swiss firm Bauart Architekten offers an answer in the form of a contemporary, pre-fab two-storey home, using an innovative concept from the Holz 2000 research project. The design, at 11 × 4.4 m (36 × 14 ft), is very compact, and can be used as an infill building or as a standalone structure. It incorporates versatility, simplicity and quick assembly to create a small home that is efficient without compromising any of its functions.

Manufactured in the factory and then transported to site, Smallhouse can be assembled in a single day, minimizing cost while delivering maximum design. The design itself used a wood-framed construction, with additional wood finishes. The final assembly is a panel-type system, developed by pre-fab specialists WeberHaus, and allows virtually any type of finishing. Although pre-fabrication methods already ensure efficient construction, the design also introduces versatility, allowing the house to grow and adapt according to the needs of its residents. The only aspects that are fixed are the panoramic windows and horizontal wood sidings. The ground plan can also be altered to form an L- or U-shaped layout to accommodate an interior atrium. Further customization is achieved by varying the grouping of the volumes, or choosing a pitched or flat roof. The house's modular construction also allows for future extensions as they become necessary over time, without difficulty.

Four generously sized windows bring in natural light – one on each side of the building, associated with the four spatial zones of the house. The house contains a living and dining room, kitchen, bathroom, gallery and hallway to connect the functions, along with two rooms – for sleeping or working – divided by a sliding wall. An awning or terrace can also be added later to expand the living space.

A wood-burning stove and electric heaters provide warmth in the kitchen and bathroom; methods that, together with the well-insulated walls, offer a constant interior temperature and do not rely on fossil fuels. As a result, the house is environmentally sustainable and heating costs are reduced.

Smallhouse's flexibility allows for customization and adaptation to modern family life. Moreover, its compact design embraces the idea that people are willing to live small and break away from the rigidity of the urban context. This pre-fabricated home is efficient in terms of its cost and construction, and also allows residents options in the choice of layout and accessories – all with the possibility of expansion in the future.

Above left
Side façade.

Above right
Front and side façades.

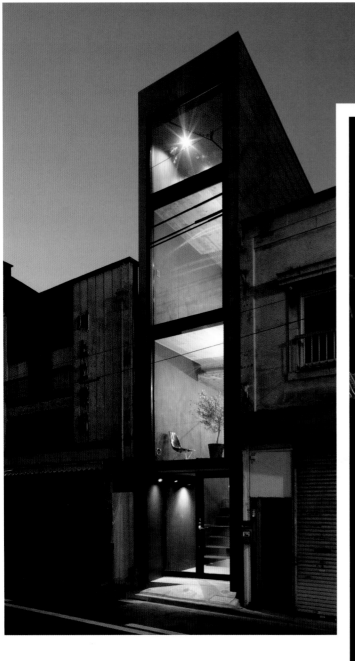

Above
Front elevation, at night.

Right
Kitchen.

narrow gains

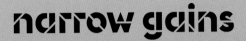

1.8m Width House
Tokyo, Japan
YUUA Architects

Designed by YUUA Architects and located in Toshima, the densest ward in central Tokyo, the four-storey 1.8m Width House is built on a site that is a mere 2.5 m (8 ft) wide and 11 m (36 ft) long. Like many Japanese cities, Tokyo has a shortage of land, and houses tend to be narrow and squeezed into the available space – hence their common description as 'eel's nests'.

The interior of the house had to be carefully planned. Split-level floors create natural divisions between the various spaces, reducing the need for walls and making the small rooms appear larger. A staircase at the back of the house connects the three upper levels, while another small stairway at the centre allows circulation between the lower floors. To maximize space, shelves line both stairs and kitchen, with open routes for pipework, which are adaptable and easy to maintain. Columns and beams are limited, and there is very little evidence of the house's steel frame on view.

Attention was also paid to the organization of the layout. Starting at the bottom, the lowest floor is used as a storage area, with the basement constructed specifically to save energy. The main entrance is located on the first split-level, which leads up to a bedroom and study space. Continuing on up, the main living area contains the kitchen, with a countertop that extends to form a dining table and a platform for a ladder leading up to the terraces on the floor above or to the rooftop. Finally, at the very top of the house are a loft bedroom and a bathroom.

It is difficult for light to penetrate into such a narrow building, so full-height windows were used at the front, overlooking the street. Towards the back of the house, two skylights illuminate the areas where natural light from the main windows cannot reach. The stairs comprise steel-tread open risers, with slender handrails that allow the light to filter through.

Right
Dining area.

Below
Stairs.

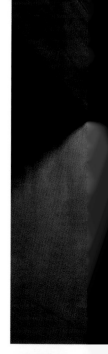

Split-level floors create natural divisions between the spaces, reducing the need for walls and making small rooms appear larger.

The dark colour scheme, created with marble-dust paint, lends depth to the interior, while the scaffolding boards used for the floors and ceilings provide texture. These boards also emphasize the building's façade and elongated windows, which create a focal point for each floor.

There are many similar sites across Japan with equally tiny footprints, which require careful consideration in the design to make these 'eel's nests' comfortable. The 1.8m Width House, with its overlapping half-levels, demonstrates that even on an extremely narrow plot, an innovative layout can provide comfort and privacy.

let there be light

Collingwood House
Melbourne, Victoria, Australia
ArchiBlox

Wishing to continue living in the centre of Melbourne, a young couple bought a home on a narrow plot of land, but once children arrived, they quickly realized they needed more space. Rather than moving to a bigger house outside of the city, however, the family decided to build a pre-fabricated home, with a total area of 70 m² (753 sq ft). As well as not having to move away from their beloved neighbourhood, the new urban infill house brought the family many other advantages.

The site was only 4.8 m (16 ft) wide, with an area of 140 m² (1,507 sq ft), making conventional methods of construction impractical. Pre-fabrication meant that the house could be built quickly, unaffected by the weather, and produce less waste. In the end, it took twenty-two weeks to build in the factory, with all of the interior details, including the copper kitchen lights, pre-installed and complete. The house was transported from the factory in Wonthaggi, 132 km (82 miles) southeast of Melbourne, as two separate components. Once the modules arrived on site, they were lifted by crane over the eight-storey Melbourne Polytechnic building.

On a typical site, assembly is generally about eight hours. In the case of Collingwood House, there was a slight delay caused by wind, but the main structure was still completed within a day, aided by the 50 to 150 mm (2 to 6 in.) tolerance to the neighbouring walls and fences, which would not have been possible if the house had been built from scratch on site. Once the structure was up, the house took another six weeks to complete.

The two-storey home comprises two bedrooms, two bathrooms and a study, in addition to the communal functions. The design also extends internal space to the outside, bringing in an abundance of light. The open plan for the living, dining and kitchen area continues out into the front garden, which is orientated to the north to allow the winter sun to heat and light the space. This, along with the large opening, provides natural ventilation during the summer. The living area opens up to another small courtyard on the western side of the house, offering a flexible family space and a generous living area. The opening to the courtyard brings even more light into the house, with room for a vertical garden along the fence for herbs and other plants.

The decision to build a pre-fabricated home enabled the family to stay in their urban location, without having to invest the time or money necessary in building a conventional house. The construction process was economical, and the passive design will save the family money over time, with energy bills reduced by a third. Sitting perfectly on its narrow site, Collingwood House will be able to be enjoyed in comfort for many years to come.

Many people prefer to live away from the bustle of the city, or have holiday homes for enjoying time in the outdoors. These residences are often built in remote locations, where labour and materials can be limited, and the surrounding ecosystem too fragile for heavy construction equipment. Traditional building practices, therefore, are both slow and costly, and as a result, make pre-fabrication strategies particularly advantageous. Modular units are delivered to site and assembled by crane, a method that is less damaging to the landscape and reduces build time considerably. Homeowners can adapt the arrangement of the units according to their own preferences, or include sustainable systems to save on energy and other costs.

COUNTRY DWELLINGS

Motives and typologies

Pre-fabricated wood-framed homes feature a wide range of compositions, from the number of floors to the allocation of spatial use. They also often have a grid-based system, with regularly shaped exterior walls.[32] But the organization of such houses need not be constrained to a standardized formula: building from pre-fab units gives clients new freedom in customizing their homes, upgrading or replacing parts over time.

The need for accuracy and connector logic in modular units does not limit the design to a rectangular form. In fact, the computer-aided process allows architects to experiment with optimal space division in a small plot. Pre-fab units can often stretch the buildable extent in a restricted space by replacing the uncertainties of labour with accurate measurements.[33] Modern sophistication in the building envelope and in mechanical systems create more variability and less chance for error during production, adding to the practical advantages of fabrication within a controlled factory environment. As designers continue to experiment with ways of reducing cost and materials while maintaining quality, they become more willing to offer pre-fabricated designs to clients.

Design and construction process

Factory-production takes up most of the time in pre-fabricated wood-framed construction. On-site assembly is minimal, as the units are approximately 95 per cent complete on arrival.[34] These modular units, which form the building blocks, are usually built in long, rectangular cubes, the most efficient shape to transport. Despite the need for larger equipment like cranes, lifting a pre-fabricated building onto site allows for safer construction on sensitive ground. There is less long-term damage, and the fast building process reduces the amount of waste. In particularly delicate natural settings, panellized systems may be used, allowing the lighter compartment units to be carried by hand over a short distance. Once on site, assembly is often relatively intuitive.

A primary goal in the building of pre-fab wood-framed rural homes is to achieve sustainability standards within a limited budget. Pre-fabricated houses permit customization at a reduced cost, with standardized modular compartments that are assembled according to the conditions of the site. The process also allows for the easier integration of advanced technologies, including passive ventilation and heating, which cuts down on utility costs. Utility bills can be as little as 40 per cent of those of neighbouring homes of a comparable size, which receive power from the same source.

Because the composition of such homes follows clear connector logic, often with a grid-based layout, the installation of natural ventilation systems into the design is encouraged. Factory-fabricated building envelopes can be constructed with SIPs and a guaranteed sealed

This type of housing has become more popular in recent years, and designers are actively looking for solutions to produce high-quality designs that are affordable. Pre-fabrication allows the integration of advanced technologies and a site-specific design that satisfies environmental standards. Such homes are also better integrated into sensitive sites, with reduced waste production and a short assembly period. Layouts often incorporate a grid-based connector and stack system, aiding in the installation of passive sustainable systems. The overall layout of the units, however, is not constrained to a standardized form. Unlike more traditional housing, pre-fab wood-framed homes feature a greater amount of flexibility in terms of the needs of the clients and of the site itself.

insulation. By deliberately placing windows and air ducts on particular walls and at certain heights, a breezeway is created across the connected spaces. Natural circulation not only brings in fresh air, but also prevents the collection of moisture and reduces the need for mechanical ventilation systems. By the same rationale, passive solar orientation, a semi-customized feature, is another common technique. The placement and orientation of windows and walls are chosen according to a house's location and solar paths at the site. A solution is found that will help keep the house warm in winter, with less reliance on heating. In the summer, the sun's height and hours of daylight are taken into account to prevent direct solar heating on the interior and keep the house cool.[35]

Water usage can be reduced in pre-fab wood-framed homes through the installation of appliances such as low-flow taps and dual-flush toilets. These houses may also feature a water-recycling system, which stores greywater from showers, sinks and washing machines and carries it through a second set of pipes to provide water for toilets and watering the lawn. Rainwater can also be collected from the roof in a cistern to fill greywater storages for a similar use.

Above left
Pre-fab interior components.

added bonus

Plus House
Tyresö, Sweden
Claesson Koivisto Rune

Located twenty minutes from Stockholm, Plus House sits in a rural setting outside the municipality of Tyresö. Pre-fabrication is a common construction method in Sweden, making up about 70 per cent of the single-family housing market, but these homes are often just steel-framed pods, which was an efficient way to build houses during the post-war period. This design, the first pre-fab home by architectural firm Claesson Koivisto Rune, is an attempt to reject the precedent of sub-par construction and to improve the aesthetics of pre-fabricated houses.

Although the architects usually avoid pitched rooflines, here they decided to combine a pitched roof with the typical proportions of a traditional Swedish barn, thus finding a new interpretation of a familiar form. The two-storey, wood-clad house has no 'traditional' windows, and instead entire lengths of the building have been glazed. The ground floor has large expanses of glass along both of its long walls, while upstairs the two gable ends are glazed, creating a feeling of spaciousness. When looking at the plan, the two sightlines through the building appear perpendicular, forming a 'plus' sign.

The house is open plan, with communal spaces on the ground floor and private areas above. To divide the space on the first floor, a central box-shaped wall wraps around the stairwell. The staircase itself has open risers, allowing views outside and natural light to filter through. All of the doors on the first floor slide open, rather than swing, to save space. A spruce deck expands indoor living to the outdoors.

To achieve a minimal footprint, the pre-fabricated wooden components – superstructure, cladding panels and decking – were made from sustainably sourced timber. Unlike traditional builds, this pre-fab house is a generic design, rather than specific to its particular site, so that it can be placed anywhere. Shade is not dependent on its orientation, therefore, and is provided by 90 cm (3 ft) overhangs on each side of the building. The house is positioned so that the sightlines through the house lead into the woods or across the nearby estuary to take advantage of the landscape.

Although the architects took inspiration from Sweden's vernacular barns, their design has a contemporary feel, and is customized by the owners with furnishings and a Japanese-style garden in front of the building. Plus House demonstrates that 'pre-fab' does not have to mean 'cookie-cutter', and that even though a design is not site-specific, orientation can still be considered for site optimization, with the residents making later modifications to create a home that is specific to them.

Left
Study.

Below
Stairs.

Opposite
Kitchen.

Left
Interior view.

Below
Side elevation.

swiss made

Zufferey House
Valais, Switzerland
Nunatak Architectes

Just north of Valais, Switzerland, is the mountain of Ardévaz, whose form and natural resources provided the inspiration for the shape and plan of Zufferey House by Nunatak Architectes. Surrounded by vineyards and looming mountains in the distance, the building resembles a block of stone, delicately balanced in an open field. In contrast to its stony appearance, the house has a wood frame, pre-fabricated for reasons that were both practical and financial.

The slope of the roof reflects the east and west faces of the mountain, and is covered in slate to further tie in with its surroundings. Beneath the upwardly tilted portion of the house, at the western end, is the entrance and space for parking. To the east and south, the terrace and garden act as extensions of the living space and provide shade and protection from the weather, especially from the wind blowing up the valley. The size and position of the windows were also deliberately chosen to take advantage of the stunning landscape.

Inside, walls are formed from a layer of particle-board panels with an insulation coat. Various arrays of slates were placed in the same orientation as the slope of the roof for exterior protection, and enormous planks of fir, kept in their natural state, were used for the roof and floor structures. The floor itself had a rough screed applied directly to the concrete, with the heating system integrated inside it, creating an 'active' slab. The sophisticated design of the building meant that materials were simplified as much as possible to reduce the cost of construction.

The house has two storeys, separated by function. The ground floor contains the social components: a spacious open kitchen, living and dining area, cloakroom and storage. Large glass doors open to extend the living space out onto a terrace and into the garden. A narrow, wooden staircase leads up to the first floor, which holds the private areas – three bedrooms and two small bathrooms – as well as an open attic space with a study and television room.

Zufferey House was designed to take advantage of the breathtaking, 360° views of the Swiss landscape. This pre-fab home was also built to withstand the elements and allow residents to enjoy the outdoors without being affected by the weather. Apart from the functionality of the structure, the house also seems to emerge from the landscape, while maintaining a connection with the mountains beyond.

Above
Side façade.

Left
Detail of the elevated portion.

Opposite
Interior stairs.

Previous pages
Side view.

boxing clever

Casa GG
Santa Maria de Palautordera, Spain
Alventosa Morell Arquitectes

Designed for a family who wanted to move out of the city, Casa GG was built with energy-efficient construction methods, a limited budget and a tight deadline. By completing the entire build in the factory, the house arrived on site without the need for later finishes. Each of the six wood-framed modules are flexible enough to adapt to the conditions of the site, and the architects also conducted a bioclimatic study and formulated design strategies to improve comfort and achieve the requirements set out by Passivhaus guidelines.

The modules were built in four months, and are relatively small owing to transportation limitations. With wood being the main material used for the structure and finishing, the work was completed by a specialized carpentry team, ensuring that manufacturing details were optimized and costs were kept low, although new construction was needed to integrate the house into its natural setting. The use of timber continues inside, with spruce chosen for the doors and architraves, and the furniture.

To reduce the building's ecological footprint, materials were all locally sourced. The design also made use of an array of breathable materials to avoid the problem of condensation, caused by temperature differences between inside and out, and concrete was used for the flooring to contrast with the lighter tone of the walls. The house has high thermal resistance and can be heated by a single radiator, resulting in a 77 per cent reduction in the energy needed for heating.

Left
Dining area.

Below
Study space.

Previous pages
Side view.

The architects conducted a bioclimatic study and formulated design strategies to achieve the requirements set out by Passivhaus guidelines.

The interstitial space joins the various components and can be adjusted by the residents as their needs evolve. It also becomes a solar collector in winter by creating a greenhouse effect, using the full-pane windows to retain warmth. In summer, the windows open up to create a covered outdoor terrace that connects to the garden, while the modules transform into roof terraces as extended outdoor living space. The front of the house contains the living room, which overlooks the garden and connects to the dining room at the centre of the plan. The two children's bedrooms protrude into the garden, with the master bedroom extending out at the rear of the building. The kitchen and bathroom are accessed via a timber-and-glass corridor.

Casa GG exploits the characteristics of wood and demonstrates energy-efficiency through the innovative placement of the windows. Along with the adaptable pre-fab modules, an interesting contrast occurs between the vertical trunks of the existing trees and the horizontal slats of this wood-framed home.

Above
Front façade, detail.

island life

Gambier Island House
Gambier Island, British Columbia, Canada
Turkel Design

Set into steep terrain overlooking the waters of Howe Sound, this remote home off the coast of British Columbia was designed for a client who wanted a getaway from the city and a place to entertain guests. The architects' TD3 2490 model was the first of their designs to be built in North America, and was suitable for the challenging location of the site, which is only accessible by water. The house received NAHB industry awards for Green-Built Home, International Single-Family, and One-of-a-Kind Home under 4,000 sq ft (or just over 1,200 m).

At the owner's request, the cedar-and-glass building was designed to have the least possible impact on the rocky shoreline, to blend inconspicuously into the landscape, and to be energy-efficient and self-sufficient during the area's prolonged power outages during the winter months. The design was modified to adapt to the steep site, and the interior layout altered to provide a passive heating/cooling envelope with sweeping views in several directions. To reduce disturbance during construction, only six trees were removed.

A dual-pitched roof promotes natural airflow and single-location rainwater collection system, while the wood construction and finishes, as well as the river-stone cladding on the flat portion of the roof, help the house blend into its surroundings. The architects used computer-aided mapping for precise placement of the building on site. The components needed to be delivered to the island by barge; following their arrival, the crew members arrived on site and completed the assembly.

Set into steep terrain overlooking Howe Sound, the house was designed as a remote getaway and a place to entertain guests.

Gambier Island House is positioned to open onto a grove of old-growth cedars and look out through the treetops to the opposite shoreline, with windows strategically placed to capture views of the forest and water. Owing to the nature of the site, the interior layout is upside-down and backwards. Since access to the site is primarily by boat, the entrance is at the lowest level of the house, facing the water. As a result, the top floor is the primary living space, which benefits from filtered sunlight as the sun moves from east to west, continually changing the ambience inside the house. The cathedral ceilings, 5.5 m (18 ft) off the ground, and large windows provide ample natural light. The open-plan design includes three bedrooms and three bathrooms, with a dining and living room surrounded by glass walls.

Although the architects' TD3 2490 model had to be modified for this project, pre-fabrication was the ideal method for precise and practical construction at a difficult and remote location. The design is green-certified, while still containing all of the features desired by the owner, and merges into the surrounding forest, which provides privacy and shade. Gambier Island House is a perfect example of the benefits and flexibility afforded by pre-fabricated homes.

Right
Living room.

Opposite
Hallway.

Previous pages
Side façade.

grand pile

Loblolly House
Taylors Island, Maryland, USA
KieranTimberlake

Set on Taylors Island along Maryland's Eastern Shore, this two-storey, pre-fab house is nestled within a forest of towering loblolly trees that line Chesapeake Bay. It is perched atop a timber foundation and is accessed via an unassuming staircase at the rear of the property. In deference to its surroundings, the house was designed for minimal environmental impact and assembled using pre-fabricated parts.

Loblolly House was also elevated to respond to the environmental conditions. A pile foundation was chosen to achieve this, with pillars driven into the ground to anchor the structure, requiring no excavation. Placed along the edges of the building and sporadically in between, these timber supports extend from the ground, creating a space beneath the house that allows for water to flow beneath it, both preventing the flooding that regularly occurs in the area and forming a sheltered space for parking.

The piles were skewed slightly to provide additional lateral support to the house. Inconspicuous among the rest, two hollow piles enclose the drinkable water, power and drainage. This type of foundation eliminates the risk of exposure to hazardous by-products generated during the construction of conventional foundations, and have minimal impact on the soil. The height given by the piles allows for distant views across the water, as well as privacy, by separating the house from the ground below. The space beneath the structure also has a panoramic view of Chesapeake Bay from the forest.

In deference to its surroundings, Loblolly House was designed for minimal environmental impact, using pre-fabricated parts.

The installation of piles is the least precise moment during construction, and can deviate significantly from the original design. To minimize delay, the foundation design was simulated prior to construction. After insertion, the piles are levelled and connected to the aluminium using engineered timber. Diverging slightly from the orthogonal, the angles of the supports follow the natural tilts of the trees; when viewed from below, the foundation appears to extend the forest floor. Although used for a purely pragmatic purpose, the piles assume a poetic role in the design as a foundation built from the forest.

Like the piles, the house echoes its natural setting, with raised slender supports, a main elevated volume and a green roof, and was designed with the same concern for environmental impact. All of the materials were supplied and produced from within an 800-km (500-mile) radius, reducing transportation. The building's constituent parts were fabricated off-site, resulting in a build that took less than six weeks.

The house can be easily disassembled, and most materials recuperated with limited waste. Any potential environmental damage caused during the build was reduced by minimizing the construction time, and since the house was built on top of a pile foundation, it can be relocated easily, allowing the property to revert quickly back to its natural state.

Left
Bedroom.

Below
Side façade, detail.

Previous pages
Kitchen and dining areas.

On pp. 116–17
Side façade.

'Plug-and-play' homes are pre-fabricated modular units that can be installed rapidly and made ready for immediate use. Unlike pre-fab houses, which require some on-site assembly and are generally permanent structures, plug-and-play versions require no assembly on delivery, and simply need to be connected to utilities. When it's time to move on, the house can come, too. Their inherent simplicity, affordability and portability, along with sustainable features, high-quality materials and cutting-edge technologies, make this type of housing an exciting alternative.

PLUG-AND-PLAY

Key design principles

The design of plug-and-play units is guided by the need for easy transportation, while limiting damage. Weight becomes a crucial factor, filtering through to many other design decisions. Units must be heavy enough to sustain maximum wind drag, but not so heavy as to exceed the supporting allowance of rooftops.[36] Weight requirements vary greatly, with some firms claiming their units are rooftop safe with an average weight of 600 lbs/linear ft (6,350 kg/m), while others make the same claim at 22 lbs/linear ft (230 kg/m) to a maximum of 80 lbs/linear ft (820 kg/m).[37] In any case, it is important to verify roof allowances and structural capacity before placing a plug-and-play home on top of a flat roof.

External building components, such as windows and doors, present a special challenge, as they can break and weaken the overall structure. Rather than limiting their number, however, designers have instead developed ways of protecting them during travel, from sliding large panels over façades made almost entirely from glass, to creating doors and windows that fold into the structure, which allow more inside space once the unit is installed. Thick shutters can also be used to seal off the glass and add structural support, much like hurricane-proof buildings. In addition, designers have proposed units that retract mechanically inward to protect them during transportation, and extend back out again at the push of a button.[38]

Because plug-and-play houses tend to be small, designers must consider carefully the interior design. The aim is to create spaces that feel large, while still being efficient and functional. Many of the concepts were covered in the chapter on narrow homes (see pp. 80–95), but there are some principles that are unique to plug-and-play structures. While transportable units have been seen as cheap and uncomfortable, recent innovations have produced high-tech, aesthetically pleasing buildings that are sleek, efficient and lightweight.[39] It is because these homes are smaller and less costly than other houses that architects are able to use more expensive materials, sophisticated technologies and customizable features to make them comfortable and suited to modern life.[40]

The idea of built-ins can be extended to the arrangement of utilities, and to save space, some designers have begun embedding heating and cooling into the floors and walls. Plug-and-play homes are typically designed so that the roof can open to let air circulate, and many units are equipped with mechanical ventilation systems.[41] Firms such as Lab Zero are also refurbishing old shipping containers to promote sustainable ideas about reuse and recycling. Some of these attempts have been extremely successful, creating architecture that is both cutting edge and environmentally conscious. Other companies are similarly targeting pre-fabrication for affordable housing that can be delivered to customers around the world, in a similar manner to, for example, the motor industry.

Design adaptations

Mobile plug-and-play homes will often share similar characteristics across different designs to facilitate their mobility and adaptability. Variations may include length, number of levels and whether or not the structure is expandable with fold-out or pop-up segments.[42] The layout, finishes and form of the roof also provide distinction. Although the sophisticated use of materials and high-tech appliances are less common, owing primarily to financial considerations, the inclusion of higher-quality fixtures and fittings could make plug-and-play homes more appealing to a larger demographic of buyers, and thus provide more developmental potential.

Moving panels, fitted furniture and multi-purpose spaces are all used to create convertible rooms that maximize small living spaces. A unique feature of plug-and-play homes is the potential to expand, accommodating comfort while satisfying the need for portability. While individual units usually take the shape of a solid rectangle for ease of shipping, once the house is in place and connected to utilities, the addition of expandable components can provide both character and additional living space.[43] Depending on the size of the units, such homes feature specially designed service areas to contain the necessary equipment for heating, cooling and electrics.[44]

dutch treat

Heijmans ONE
Amsterdam, Netherlands
MoodBuilders

The Netherlands has been experiencing a shortage of rental housing, as well as a surfeit of derelict sites. In addition, the number of single people in their mid-twenties to mid-thirties, who earn too much for social housing but not enough for the free-rental sector, is expected to become larger than the population of Rotterdam by 2050. In response, Dutch firm MoodBuilders have designed Heijmans ONE to meet the demand for rental housing that is both individual and affordable.

The design is a two-storey, single-person home with all the necessary facilities, and can be fully installed in a single day. These reusable, sustainable houses have a lifespan of twenty-five to thirty years, and can be placed on prime urban locations without a permanent commitment to the site or the accompanying high rent, as well as on derelict sites, thus providing a temporary solution until the land is ready to be developed.

Each home has a kitchen, bathroom, living area, separate bedroom and a small patio. Once on site, it is connected to the mains for water, sewage and electricity. It also has photovoltaic panels integrated into the roof for generating energy. The solid-wood skeleton, recycled wood façade and all-electric system make the homes even more energy-efficient. Since each unit is built with the utilities connections pre-installed, they can be easily transported to different sites with pre-existing facilities. The target residents are young adults who would otherwise have to settle for a small, expensive apartment, live in a flatshare or move back in with their parents.

As a result, the houses are varied slightly so that each one is clearly recognizable, giving a sense of individuality and independence. The ground-floor module links to the asymmetrical roof module above, which itself creates a diverse 'roofscape'. The home also has a ceiling height of 5.9 m (19 ft), allowing for plenty of natural light. It is compact, but spacious enough for a large living area and a bedroom on the mezzanine, which can hold a double bed.

With the average length of a lease around five years, depending on the landowner and city regulations, Heijmans ONE both offers a solution for young people who want their own home and enables neglected urban areas to become more dynamic. The architects' ultimate aim is to create homes that are more sustainable by being self-supporting. International interest in the project means that there is also the potential to expand to other demographics and regions.

Right
Rear view.

Opposite
Living area.

Previous page
Front view.

Installation of module.

tiny house

Sonoma weeHouse
Santa Rosa, California, USA
Alchemy Architects

Designed in Minnesota, built in Oregon and delivered
to a client in California, Sonoma weeHouse is a small,
ultra-minimal home designed by Geoffrey C. Warner of
Alchemy Architects and customized in collaboration with
the client, himself a designer. The project comprises two
pre-fabricated, open-sided boxes set on concrete plinths,
nestled in the hills outside Santa Rosa, California.

For ease of transport, the house was designed in two
parts – a main box and a porch – and shipped more or less
complete, before being cantilevered onto site. The living
module features a kitchen, sleeping area, living space and
bath, with a bed box in whitewashed oak sitting in the
middle of the volume separating the living space
and bathroom. The porch was bolted onto the main box
to extend 3 m (10 ft) out into the landscape. The separate
guest house is an abridged version of the main house,
with a wardrobe, also in whitewashed oak, forming the
bathroom wall to create privacy and storage. Clad in
corrugated steel, both house and guest house feature
steel frames, sliding-glass walls and ipe interiors, and
are positioned to make the most of the dramatic views
of the Californian wine country.

Sonoma weeHouse is a response to the current
popular fascination with 'tiny houses', industrial tech,
simplicity and sustainable living, and an efficient yet
celebratory use of materials. Two new designs being
beta-tested by Alchemy Architects are Barn House, a
SIPs kit that combines 'farm-tech' with modern design,
and Light House, a SIPs kit mobile hotel.

Sonoma weeHouse is a response to the current fascination with 'tiny houses', and is an efficient yet celebratory use of materials.

Above
View from deck.

Right
Front view.

Previous pages
View of interior.

Above
Rear façade.

Left
Interior.

movable feast

Casa Transportable
Spain
Ábaton Arquitectura

The APH80 series was developed by Spanish firm Ábaton Arquitectura as an ideal home for two that could be easily transported and placed on site. It embodies the architects' principles of wellbeing, environmental balance and simplicity. The team conducted a thorough study that set out the desired proportions and functions of the house, incorporating simple yet sturdy construction and carefully chosen materials. As a result, their thoughtful design has endless functional possibilities, from guest house to office or holiday home.

The architects' demand for sustainability is applied to each of their projects. Here, wood has been used throughout: it is hypo-allergenic and fosters a feeling of serenity, and has been sourced from a managed forest that will regrow to provide further carbon storage, oxygen generation and habitat preservation. The monolithic exterior is created by grey cement boards that cover the façade, which is wrapped in 12 cm (5 in.)-thick thermal insulation. For the interior, Spanish fir trees, dyed white, form the panelling, while the triple glazing with low emissivity has a low heat transmission of 1.4 kilowatts. The use of CNC (computer numerical controlled) modelling in the manufacturing process ensured precision, and most of the materials used can be recycled.

Inside are three distinct spaces: a combined living room and kitchen, bathroom and double bedroom. The rectangular interior was designed to be roomy enough to accommodate two people comfortably, yet small enough to be transported on the back of a lorry. The gabled roof

Right
Side façade.

Below
Living/kitchen area.

Previous pages
Side view.

hard enough, there is no need for traditional foundations; otherwise, geological tests must be conducted to define the appropriate foundations. Other optional installations include a water tank, septic tank and solar panels.

The life expectancy of homes in the APH80 series are comparable to conventional housing, with certain high-quality components being even more durable. The modular system can be customized by combining features from other series, and the units are also expandable in height and width. The architects are planning to develop the series further, with larger spaces and greater versatility.

Casa Transportable embodies the architects' principles of wellbeing, environmental balance and simplicity.

allows a ceiling height of 3.5 m (11 ft 6 in.) at its highest point, and wall panels pivot open to reveal sliding-glass doors at the front and windows to the side. The large sliding-glass doors bring the outdoors in, and allow the home to blend into its surroundings. The furniture is by Spanish brand Batavia.

The APH80 series is designed and manufactured entirely in Spain. Construction in the factory is six to eight weeks, and the house is delivered to site in one piece. The pre-fabricated elements can be assembled within a day, after which water, electricity and plumbing are connected. Ideally, the utility connections would already exist on site; if there are no existing connections, however, the architects can provide self-sufficient solutions. The design can be installed almost anywhere, as long as the site is accessible by flatbed lorry and crane. If the ground is

Above left
Side façade.

Below
Bedroom.

Right
Living area.

Although the definition of 'mid-rise' when applied to apartment buildings varies, it is generally accepted to mean those between four and twelve storeys in height, a range that allows such buildings to be more easily integrated into existing communities in smaller cities. Using pre-fab systems would make the process even easier, and would minimize disruption on site. And by including a variety of unit typologies, these mid-rise buildings would also be able to meet the needs of a wider range of residents. Along with sustainable building materials, energy-saving technologies and public-transportation planning, they have the potential to offer greater comfort and reduced energy costs.

APARTMENT BUILDINGS

Advantages of mid-rise buildings

As the global population continues to rise, along with more and more urban settlements around the world, it is clear that the sustainable management of cities is of paramount importance. Although a high percentage of urban residents live in 'mega-cities' of ten million or more, these are not the cities that are growing most rapidly.[45]

Along with increasing sustainability, mid-rise apartment buildings can also offer mixed-use and mixed-density living for a wider range of living situations and demographics. A variety of unit types that would accommodate different family types and needs could exist within one complex, for example, with the ground floor offering retail space and other amenities to residents and the wider community. This arrangement could potentially increase walkability in the area and put more people close to public transportation, while also offering convenience and supporting local businesses.[46]

Method of assembly

Pre-fabrication strategies can offer significant advantages, from the precision of factory-controlled construction to less material waste and time needed for assembly on site. One of two methods are generally used in mid-rise buildings: a panellized system, or a modular one. Panellized buildings are typically constructed from SIPs, made by pressing foam insulation between two outer panels of plywood or oriented strand board (OSB).

Sections are transported by lorry to site, occasionally with windows and doors in place – if the necessary protective measures have been taken before shipment. This type of system needs to be connected to services and utilities once constructed, which can take time.[47]

With modular construction, buildings are made from an assembly of modules – typically in box shapes – which are produced in factories using assembly-line techniques. The modules have finishes, flooring, and even utilities in place, before being shipped to site. With either system, once the pre-fabricated components arrive, they are hoisted into place by crane to match a pre-measured foundation or location. One advantage of the modular system, especially in the case of apartment buildings, is the faster build time – it takes longer for workers to correctly assemble the various panels on site than it does to place modules. More manual labour means more cost. Modules can also be placed in a variety of configurations, giving greater flexibility to the layout design.

Variability of design

One challenge frequently faced with any type of pre-fab construction is how to design a building so that it does not appear repetitive or monotonous. This becomes especially important for larger buildings such as apartment blocks, as their façades have a considerable effect on the streetscape and the overall feeling of the neighbourhood. If designers are conscientious with their decisions, they

can help change preconceived notions associated with
pre-fabricated buildings.[48] Design strategies to help
break up the repetitive appearance of pre-fab structures
can be aesthetic decisions, or the result of the form of
the structure itself. If buildings are built with modules,
adjustments to the design of the assembly of units can
result in some interestingly stacked forms, and variations
in materials, colours and façade elements such as
balconies, roof types and shutters can also help to make
buildings eye-catching and appealing from street level.
Keeping these considerations in mind during the decision-
making process will go far in reducing the stigma attached
to pre-fabricated design.

Variability can also be introduced into the interiors
of pre-fab mid-rise apartment buildings by providing a
range of different unit types. Designers can produce a
series of typologies for modules of different sizes, from
micro-units for singles and couples to more expansive
multi-bedroom units for families. They then only need to
decide how to arrange the units to create an interesting
and efficient layout. By offering different unit typologies,
apartment buildings are better able to provide for a wide
range of demographics, lifestyles and socio-economic
backgrounds, and therefore become more socially
sustainable.[49] The concept of social sustainability can be
pushed even further by providing lifestyle considerations
such as live/work units or aging-in-place potential for
the elderly.[50]

Below
Courtyard.

modular model

Moho
Manchester, UK
ShedKM

Moho – an abbreviation of 'modular housing' – by UK firm ShedKM (see also Town House; p. 56) puts into practice the principles of the 1998 Egan Report by applying the idea of pre-fabricated apartment buildings to the private sector for the first time. The seven-storey building contains 102 fully furnished flats of varying sizes and typologies, above shops and parking spaces, with each apartment condensed into a single volumetric module and swivelled 90° to maximize window frontage.

Offering compact, high-quality accommodation, the scheme is aimed at first-time buyers. Each apartment, containing one to three bedrooms, was pre-fabricated as single volumetric module at a plant in York, fully fitted with kitchen, bathroom and storage, along with slimline wall-mounted electric panel heaters. The modules were built as robust, steel-framed structures with enclosing floors and walls in combinations of steel sheets, particle board and plasterboard, with each taking eighteen working days to build, before being transported to site. Spine-access cores were introduced as independent structures between the stacks of self-supporting modules.

The high-density, hemmed-in site in the centre of Manchester also posed a challenge. The design of the whole project is U-shaped and backs onto a similarly shaped scheme by a different developer, which shares the central courtyard. Each module is orientated to enjoy views to the east, west or south, and look out onto the street or a new private landscaped courtyard. The varying sizes were made possible by a series of additional clip-

on components, comprising balconies, dining pods and further bedrooms. The apartments all have floor-to-ceiling glazing, so that the living areas feel spacious, with plenty of natural light. The usable space extends out onto the balcony, which also provides shade for the apartment below. Bedrooms have a Middle Eastern-style outer screen of timber slats, separating them from the continuous balcony and creating a balance between privacy and view.

The kitchens, bathrooms and storage areas were inspired by yacht design, with the kitchen and bathroom forming a central island, and the storage space hidden behind two sliding doors in corners off the bedroom and rear hallway. Each unit in the Moho project has three bays; together, the apartments form a Cubist aesthetic that embraces the modular construction. The compact and affordable units are the result of the architects' continuing experiment with construction, which has produced a design that is out of the ordinary.

The seven-storey Moho project applies the idea of pre-fab apartment buildings to the private sector for the first time.

urban heights

The Stack
New York, New York, USA
Gluck+

The Stack is the first pre-fab, multi-unit residential building in New York, and addresses the need for moderate-income housing in the city. It is also a pilot project for developing an economically viable solution for strategically rebuilding and filling gaps in outmoded housing. To achieve this, architectural firm Gluck+ turned to pre-fab construction, as off-site manufacturing has the potential to accelerate the building schedule, shorten the financing period and turn risky sites into opportunities.

The seven-storey building was designed initially according to residents' needs, and then 'cut' into pieces that could be manufactured in a factory in Pennsylvania. During fabrication, the foundation and infrastructure were built on site. A steel column grid structure was built on top of the poured-in-place foundation to receive the modules and allow for wider spans for commercial premises. Although there was a short delay when the Department of Buildings asked to review the permits, the build time was still shorter than it would have been with conventional construction. Eventually, the off-site modules and on-site preparations came together for a four-week period of installation. A small team of eight bolted the modules in place, connected the utilities and added finishing touches, before securing the façade to the side of the building.

With the ground floor reserved for commercial use, the six storeys above were kept for residential use. In total, fifty-six modules were used to create twenty-eight units, comprising six studios, six one-bedroom, fourteen two-bedroom and two three-bedroom apartments. The

Off-site manufacturing has the potential to accelerate the building schedule and turn risky sites into opportunities.

individual units are articulated, but can be read together as a whole, while different combinations provide structural integrity and a range of layouts. When the modules are stacked together and lined up, they create an open, flexible floorplan that can be customized by inserting interior partitions.

The building as a whole is designed for durability and elegance, with sealed concrete floors, high-performance aluminium windows and tenant-controlled heating and air-conditioning. Kitchens have Corian countertops with undermounted sinks and maple cabinetry, stainless-steel appliances and WaterSense fixtures, and there is access to a communal outdoor terrace, as well as additional private terrace space for 35 per cent of the units, along with a 'virtual doorman' who greets residents upon entry to ensure their safety. The location, too, is convenient, with easy access to parks, public transportation and major roads.

During construction, The Stack functioned almost as a work of art, capturing the imagination of the neighbourhood as locals could watch the progress of the building before their eyes. As a result of the success of this residential pre-fab, the architects are exploring other options in modular construction, using The Stack as a case-study for future projects.

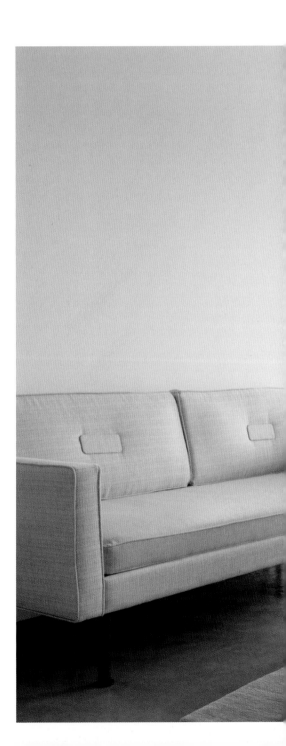

Right
Kitchen.

Below
Living room.

Pre-fab strategies, together with sustainable recycling initiatives in the building industry, have brought about a new trend in architecture: the re-purposing of steel shipping containers into modular building components. These durable building blocks can be used to create simple structures for a variety of applications, from homes to offices or temporary event venues. The standardization of modules allows for rapid shipment and quick assembly on site, while innovations in design have shown that it is possible to create attractive, comfortable homes with recycled materials. The affordable price tag also makes the humble container an attractive stepping stone, as clients can choose basic finishes to keep costs down or opt for high-end ones.

SHIPPING CONTAINERS

From container to architecture

The practice of using shipping containers can be traced back to the Second World War, when the US Army saw them as a solution to logistical problems in crisis areas. In 1956, the trucking giant Malcolm McLean developed them further in the form of 10.7 m (35 ft)-long boxes, which could be easily loaded onto ships. As the use of containers grew, their construction became standardized.[51] Widths are fixed at 2.4 m (8 ft), but height and length can vary. The two most popular models are 6 and 12 m (20 and 40 ft) long, with height ranging from the 'standard' cube (2.6 m; 8 ft 6 in.) to the 'low' (2.4 m; 8 ft) and 'high' (2.9 m; 9 ft 6 in) versions.[52] Standardization has also led to changes in transportation and lifting equipment.

The majority of shipping containers are made from slow-rusting Corten steel, which was designed to eliminate the need for painting, as a stable rusted appearance forms after the material has been exposed to weather.[53] The appeal of converting shipping containers into buildings stems from their inherent modular quality and a desire to build more conscientiously and sustainably. Added benefits such as low cost, quick construction time and easy transportation and assembly also make shipping-container homes an attractive option.

Advantages of using containers

A major incentive for the re-purposing of shipping containers into architecture is economic. In comparison to more traditional building materials, containers are inexpensive. Depending on the location of the buyer and the condition of the container, a 6 m (20 ft)-long standard cube can be purchased in the region of $1,500 to $3,500, or just over £1,200 to £1,700.[54] The popularity of secondhand shipping containers has created an expansive service network, with guarantees on quality and easy delivery.

Condition – and cost – is often dependent on the number of shipments a container has made in its lifetime. The best is a 'One Trip' container, which has only been used for a one-way journey and is sold at its first destination in near-perfect condition. 'Cargo-worthy' (CWO) containers are those that have performed several shipments and may show some wear and tear, including minor dents. Another considerable advantage of using containers for construction is their ability to be used as building modules. Their growing popularity and standardized sizes have ensured that various forms of transportation have been developed to transport them more easily.

Types of converted container architecture

To satisfy basic living needs, a shipping container must be modified to accommodate insulation and windows and doors; if more than one container is to be used, space must also be made for corridors and stairways. The advantage of this flexible, accessible mobile building

system is best seen in temporary buildings, but its application can extend to private homes, public buildings, offices, commercial premises, event venues, and more.[55] The most popular method of construction is to use the container as a spatial building module. In 1986, John M. DiMartino patented the Modular Container Building System, formed of modular shipping containers, with each unit having a specific building environment function. When the units are structurally supported, vertically mounted and horizontally connected, a complete building could then be formed. The container acts as a vessel surrounding a practical and usable amount of space, defining the spatial boundary between inside and out.[56]

During the design process, a container can be seen as a single-room building block, with one or more blocks arranged to form flexible, multi-room systems. This spatial system is inherent to the modular layout of the containers, which allows for relatively little freedom. To increase variety, it is possible to also consider negative space by removing a container from the layout. The drawback

in doing so is that the horizontal and vertical weight distribution of the container boxes through the corner joints must be correctly accounted for.[57]

Although shipping containers themselves are relatively inexpensive as building modules, their conversion to architecture can become costly if proper considerations are not made. The amount and quality of fine finishes that can be applied tend to be dictated by financial constraints, so containers are more often used for temporary structures that require less detail.

hope and glory

Containers of Hope
San Jose, Costa Rica
Benjamin Garcia Saxe

Located outside San Jose, the Containers of Hope by Costa Rican architect Benjamin Garcia Saxe were built for a family who dreamed of living somewhere they could enjoy the landscape and be with their horses, while still being only twenty minutes away from the city. Although the size of the home was not an issue, the limited budget made realizing their dream difficult. But the bold decision to explore the possibilities of building with re-purposed shipping containers allowed the family to build their new home at a much lower cost.

When designing the house, it was important for the architect to provide the family with views of the sunrise and sunset, as well as spectacular vistas of the landscape, while also creating the feelings of comfort and home. The house comprises two 12 m (40 ft)-long shipping containers, set apart from each other and linked by a central corridor with a raised roof and clerestory. The metal used for the roof was reused from sections that were removed to create the windows – large portions of the exterior walls were replaced with glazing to bring in natural light and provide views of the landscape. The containers sit on a pier foundation, reducing their impact on the site.

Since shipping containers were intended for transporting or storing objects, rather than people, the architect had to come up with a thoughtful design for transforming the space for human occupation. When entering the home, visitors have a clear view down the central corridor to a window at the far end, and the raised

roof above the corridor also creates a sense of openness, while providing cross-ventilation. As a result, the natural cooling provided when the clerestory windows are open is enough to ensure the family does not need to turn on the air-conditioning. To create a further feeling of spaciousness, the living area, which comprises the kitchen, dining and living spaces, is open plan. The master bedroom, with its roomy walk-in closet, is at the rear of the house; a smaller bedroom is next to the entrance. The bathroom is located in the master bedroom and can only be accessed through it.

With this design, Garcia Saxe has transformed sharp-edged metal shipping containers into a comfortable home that is far removed from its original characteristics. The overall cost of the house, surprisingly, was less than the price of the social housing provided for the country's poorest residents. Using shipping containers could be a method for addressing the need for more cheap housing in Costa Rica. The project also demonstrates ways of recycling old shipping containers that pose questions regarding their disposal, and uses passive alternatives to temperature control to adapt to the region's intense tropical climate.

Left
View to the outdoors.

Below
Side view.

Far left
View of the site.

Previous page
Entrance.

ship shape

Seatrain
Los Angeles, California, USA
Office of Mobile Design

Seatrain was built on an infill site next to the Brewery Art
Colony, an enclave of residences and artists' studios in the
Lincoln Heights area of Los Angeles. Its creative application
of reused commercial and industrial waste gives this urban
dwelling a unique identity. Recycled structural elements
include shipping containers, grain trailers, steel beams and
cladding, wood joists and glass. By using locally salvaged
waste, the consumption of raw materials and greenhouse
gas emissions was minimized, while building with modular
elements further reduced time and cost.

The containers were chosen for their durability,
but the modular construction also allowed for flexibility
in the design and easy disassembly in the future. The
process was a collaborative effort between client and
material fabricators to make on-site structural and artistic
adjustments. Each space is distinct: the containers hold
the master bedroom, while the exterior lap pool, extending
into the garden, was made from a grain trailer. The team
also created an interior koi pond, next to the living area,
providing a visual continuation from one to the other.
The contrast between the different materials, from the
corrugated metal sheets to the exposed wooden beams,
generates a dynamic visual and tactile experience.

At each side of the north–south axis, two containers
were stacked on top of one another to create separate
living, working, service and private areas. Recycled carpet
was also used. Owing to the modularity of the containers,
the rooms can be arranged and adapted according to
individual needs, creating a pleasing spatial fluidity.

Above
View of the entrance.

Left
Living area.

Previous pages
View from the yard.

desert oasis

Tim Palen Studio at Shadow Mountain
San Bernardino, California, USA
Ecotech Design

This prototype hybrid house by Ecotech Design, near Joshua Tree, California, is the first re-purposed container home permitted and built in the Mojave Desert. It combines various pre-engineered building and energy-conservation features to maximize efficiency, and was built at half the cost of other local pre-fabricated homes, which exceed California's strict energy-code requirements. The result is an architecturally flexible building that adapts to the extreme desert conditions.

Tim Palen Studio at Shadow Mountain comprises six recycled shipping containers, each 6 m (20 ft) long, which were fabricated and finished in Los Angeles. The modules were then transported to site, where they were stacked in pairs. All of the site work, including the foundations and utility connections, was done on location while the containers were being put in place, making this an efficient method of construction for the remote site. Five of the six containers contain the living areas, one bedroom, a studio, a bathroom and cloakroom. The other forms an appendage to the studio, and holds photographic equipment. One side of the studio is lit by six dimmable solar tubes, while on the other light is provided by a tall slit window in the stairwell, clad in corrugated recycled steel. The stairwell is also used as an art gallery.

The project incorporates other sustainable features, including a living-roof system of movable, bolt-on modules, which use greywater irrigation and are planted with native desert plants and sedums to absorb carbon dioxide, heat and glare. Recycled steel was also used,

including the six re-purposed shipping containers, a Butler pre-engineered building, solar shade canopy and an integrated steel-framing system. This amount of steel provides extraordinary strength and earthquake, fire and wind protections, and allows for large openings for natural light and ventilation.

A recycled tank harvests over 11,000 litres (2,400 gallons) of rainwater from the roof for watering the plants; another larger tank is used as a backup source of water in the event of a fire. The building incorporates rigid-foam insulation in certain areas of the walls and roof, as well as heat-treated, low-emission, double-glazed windows. For additional heating and cooling, the house is equipped with a mini-split heat pump system, and to partially deflect the desert sun, a steel Unistrut structure has been bolted to the outside to secure a skin of modular perforated metal panels. These transparent panels cover the southern, western and breezeway portions of the building. As a result of the careful design and product selection, the house exceeds current California energy-code requirements by 50 per cent.

Even in these remote desert conditions, the architects have managed to build their design efficiently and with high environmental sustainability, all at a reduced cost. The Tim Palen Studio points to the potential for expanding the scope of living in extreme conditions, and provides an excellent setting for the residents to carry out their creative work in comfort.

Above
Kitchen.

Left
Entrance area.

Opposite
Bedroom.

Previous pages
Side view.

Above
Living area.

Right
Side view.

love in a box

Containerlove
Kall, Germany
LHVH Architekten

Containerlove is a private home located on a rural site in Germany, surrounded by cow pastures and woodland. In contrast to its bucolic setting, the house has the appearance of a temporary structure. But despite the monochromatic, linear exterior, the resemblance to a shipping container ends upon stepping inside. The interior is warm and inviting, with a floorplan that, although limited by the sizes of the modules, has been optimized with a clever layout.

After a period of detailed planning, the production of the house took only four weeks, after which the pre-fabricated components were delivered to site and assembled. Since the majority of these, with the exception of a few locally made items, were completed in a factory setting, the only work to be done on site was to fit the joints, piping and connections. But although the building was complete and the clients could move in within one day, the addition of a further roof was undetermined.

Three containers of varying length were positioned to form an L-shaped floorplan, creating a spacious interior that maximizes the efficient use of the volumes, with thick walls containing an effective amount of insulation, as well as a feeling of airiness. The master bedroom and bathroom are at one end of the house; at the other, where two containers are doubled up to form a wider space, is another bedroom, along with an open office that can be used as a third bedroom by adding a partition. The kitchen/living/dining space sits between these two private spaces, at the 'elbow' of the house.

The main entrance, with a small covered porch, is located in the space between the combined living area. Five additional doorways connect inside and out, and large windows are placed strategically throughout to provide natural lighting, while also ensuring privacy. A small wooden terrace at the inside corner of the 'L' also offers some privacy and provides an outdoor living space with a view. Outside is a narrow bed of small rocks, with the rest of the site planted with grass or landscaped with larger rocks and gardens.

In this rural location, the neighbours were astonished by the sudden appearance of a house made from shipping containers. Although the design does not conform to the traditional architecture of the area, Containerlove has received positive local response. It demonstrates a well-designed plan for a spacious and comfortable layout, made possible by a pre-fabrication process that enabled an efficient, economical means of delivering the house to its countryside setting.

Left
Elevations and deck area.

Right
Living room.

Below
Front façade.

Opposite
Hallway and living area.

The emergence of new family types with new sets of requirements, along with economic and environmental concerns, have led designers to rethink the traditional, often repetitive interior layouts of homes. Rather than moving or renovating when a house becomes too small or unsuitable, pre-fabricated adaptable interiors can provide the flexibility to stay in the same home, thus removing the stress of house-hunting or intrusive building works. Adaptable interiors make use of innovative strategies such as movable partitions, modular furniture and carefully designed circulation and storage to best meet the needs of residents as they evolve over time.

ADAPTABLE INTERIORS

A need for interior flexibility

Fundamental changes in society over the last five decades or so have led to a radical shift in the way people live and form households, work and relax, grow old and die.[58] To accommodate fluctuations in circumstance, people must choose between moving or improving their homes. Some will opt to alter their houses because of the high cost and stress associated with moving. For those who stay put, few will be satisfied with their homes without some alteration, and most houses do not have the flexibility necessary to keep up with residents' changing needs.

Pre-fabricated adaptable units make use of design concepts and technologies to create an environment in which modifying a house takes precedence over demolishing it or moving somewhere else.[59] One way of achieving a flexible layout is to create a structure that requires little or no internal support.[60] This can be done by designing a narrow house with floor joists that span between the two exterior longitudinal walls, or using I-beams or open-web wood joists, which allow greater spanning distances. Creating such large, open floor spaces allows for maximum adaptability.

Once the floor is built, the space itself must be arranged to accommodate a variety of activities, including seating, working and sleeping. It needs to be as large and as square as possible to expand adaptability options. Rooms of 3.7 × 3.7 m (12 × 12 ft) to 4.6 × 4.6 m (15 × 15 ft) should be big enough to accommodate any future adaptations. It is also important that these multi-purpose areas contain no defining features, like closets, which tend to limit their overall adaptability. It is possible to use an accessible feeder pipe for electrical outlets. In such spaces, outlets must be placed either along the walls or within the floor, as building regulations prohibit their placement in demountable partitions.[61]

Types of pre-fab interiors

Homes can be built and sold with only a few enclosed rooms; over time, however, additional partitioning may become necessary. With the current method of building partition walls, such changes are expensive and disruptive. Walls developed for use in office buildings offer easy solutions, but at present, pre-fabricated walls code-approved for commercial use are permitted for residential use only in certain jurisdictions.

There are three basic types of demountable wall systems. The first is a mobile, or operable, system, with a sliding mechanism that allows a wall panel to move along ceiling tracks. The second is a demountable system, similar in concept to the traditional dry-wall system. Walls are constructed with metal studs placed at specific intervals, and pre-finished gypsum wallboards are fixed with special slips to the metal frame. The third type is the portable partition system, made from pre-fabricated panels, which are held in place by channels in the ceiling and floor.[62]

Another option is the sliding screen, a space-dividing method common in Japan, in which large screens made from paper and wooden frames are moved along tracks fixed to the floor and ceiling. In Western homes, where floor tracks are uncommon, similar screens could be developed to run along the ceiling. Sliding screens can be seen as large doors that create spaces without taking up vast amounts of floor space. While such screens provide useful visual dividers, they are not soundproof and should not be used in areas that need quiet.

Furniture partitions work in several ways to increase the efficiency and comfort of smaller homes. Using shelving and furniture to divide spaces reduces the need for interior walls, and helps make small spaces feel larger by blurring the boundaries between them and preventing rooms from feeling boxed in. Shelves or cabinets can be used to create partitions, providing much-needed storage space. Furniture partitions also make spaces more versatile, as they can be moved easily to change the size and function of a room.

Built-in storage is best suited for smaller spaces, and creates a seamless, clutter-free look.[63] Freestanding wardrobes and chests of drawers eat into floor space and make circulation routes awkward. But bespoke built-in furniture is expensive and can inhibit a room's adaptability. To maximize storage possibilities and minimize costs, a compromise between these two options is best.

Above
**Furniture House 5,
USA, Shigeru Ban and
Dean Maltz.**

flexible living

Adaptable House
Nyborg, Denmark
Henning Larsen and GXN

Adaptable House is one of six developments that comprise the MiniCO$_2$ project by Danish architectural firm Henning Larsen, together with GXN. Each of the houses illustrate various aspects of the reduction of CO$_2$ emissions in their construction, operation and maintenance. This example focuses on adaptability and examines how a flexible design can reduce the amount of materials used and CO$_2$ produced. Studies show that roughly two-thirds of families in Denmark move to a new home in the same neighbourhood, as their circumstances change. This design offers an adaptable home that is as dynamic as the family who will live in it.

Over the years, families grow or shrink, people get older, or a workspace might become necessary. In this design, there are many functional possibilities, owing to its built-in flexibility. On the ground floor, only the exterior walls are load-bearing, so that the interior walls can function like movable cabinets, and be repositioned to form one to four rooms. All of the cabling runs in an aluminium cable duct, replacing traditional skirting boards, making it possible to site electrical sockets where they are most needed. The modular design also allows for an easy addition of new entrances on the façade. Using sliding walls, the kitchen can either be closed off or connected to the dining and/or living room. These modifications are possible because the components are fabricated in standard sizes and materials. These components can be disassembled, or the entire house expanded, without damaging the existing elements.

A family living in the Adaptable House will generate twenty-six less tons of CO_2 than one living in a more conventional building. The design offers comfortable levels of ventilation, light, noise and temperature, improving both energy-efficiency and privacy, and reduces the burden of having to move because of changing needs, rather than a desire to leave the neighbourhood. It is also infinitely adaptable without the purchase of new materials – a situation that is beneficial to both the homeowners and the environment.

off the grid

Grid House
Minas Gerais, Brazil
FGMF Arquitetos

Located in a valley, and surrounded by a lush rainforest, Grid House is described by its architects as an 'inhabitable garden'. The site sits at the junction of two natural paths, one leading into the heart of the forest, the other to the top of a hill with a breathtaking view of the landscape, with the building extending over the hillside, allowing residents to walk beneath it or on top of the green roof.

The design is the result of two guiding principles: to provide privacy and a direct relationship with the land, and to take into account the area's high humidity. Since the house is two hours away from São Paulo, much thought was given to reducing the environmental impact of the construction process. A wooden grid is formed by modules supported by concrete pillars, which rise from the ground. To reduce the number of pillars and provide wider openings, 11 m (36 ft)-long trussed beams were placed at every other module, resulting in a mix of closed volumes and empty spaces.

The different areas of the home are connected by a deck, and some through the interior. In addition to the client's apartment, the house has a wash area, living space, guest room and three isolated modules, each containing two bedrooms for the children. The empty modules emphasize the structural continuity, and enhance the openings through which the garden can be glimpsed. They also provide a fragmented organization of the programme, further protecting the privacy of the inhabitants. The grid layout and modular construction mean that additional units can easily be added later.

Left
Dining area.

Below
View of living space.

Right
View of the deck.

Previous pages
Side view.

To ensure the house would not disrupt its surroundings, the architects incorporated a number of sustainable features. Pillars were used only where necessary, both to respect the terrain and to reduce the overall footprint. As a result, the house's careful placement has minimal interference below ground, allowing for water drainage and absorption. The raised structure also provides a more comfortable internal environment and avoids deterioration of materials. The Corten steel is recyclable and maintenance-free, and local materials, such as the rocks removed during the preparation of the foundations, were reused. Other materials include bamboo flooring, paint-free wall finishings and local granite.

To reduce the weight of the building, walls were made from light cement foam, with good thermal and acoustic performance capabilities. Large glass doors and windows provide views across the picturesque landscape, and help to heat the house and ventilate it. The green roof offers a path for crossing the valley, and retains the passive heat gained in winter, while preventing retention of excess heat during the summer. With its wood modules appearing to merge with the landscape, Grid House demonstrates a building's ability to embrace living in nature without disturbing it.

Outdoor area.

switch gears

Switch
Tokyo, Japan
Yuko Shibata Office

When Tokyo architect Yuko Shibata and her husband bought an aging apartment, they wanted to remodel it as a home office for Shibata's firm. The couple also wanted to create a 'switch' between home life and work life. The transformation of the residential space was deemed impossible, owing to the box-frame reinforced concrete construction, and the fact that nearly every wall was load-bearing. But although the conditions were challenging, after some renovations, the project was completed while maintaining a low price point.

The inspiration for the design came from *fusuma*, the sliding paper screens that divide or expand rooms in traditional Japanese homes. Instead of putting her office in a dedicated corner of the apartment, Shibata utilized the entire living space by cutting holes into walls and adding partitions. Plywood doors with built-in shelves open into the bedroom to form a reading nook, and two built-in bookshelves – each with large doors – were also added to create one versatile space that could change from home to office, or office to home, without altering the original floorplan. The bright-green colour chosen for the walls also helps to make the spaces appear larger than they actually are.

The first of the two bookshelves was added to the original meeting room. By repositioning the door, the space could be divided in two, so that the space on the side of the bookshelf becomes a library/meeting area. The second bookshelf was added to the bedroom, and swings open to create a passage that makes it possible to approach the

shelf from the office side without having to go through the bedroom. When the door is opened, a partition is created between the bedroom and study, making space for a library. Creating partitions that slide over the dining table or doors that open to reveal bookshelves has in turn created a more efficient use of space. When the bedroom is not in use, it can become the workroom, or the kitchen can be converted into a meeting room. By avoiding the restrictions imposed by the load-bearing walls and keeping the original structure of the apartment, including the plumbing and wiring, costs were kept to a minimum.

The design of Switch demonstrates a simple and efficient way of quickly converting a small residential unit into an office during the day, reducing the cost of renting in such a highly dense, expensive city as Tokyo.

The inspiration for the design came from *fusuma*, the sliding paper screens that divide or expand rooms in Japanese homes.

Above
Dividing wall.

Right
Study area with movable wall.

Previous pages and opposite
Swinging library wall.

past masters

Furniture House 5
Long Island, New York, USA
Shigeru Ban and Dean Maltz

Well known internationally for projects that make use of environmentally sensitive and recycled materials, Pritzker Prize-winning architect Shigeru Ban has also been working on a series of 'furniture houses' in Japan and the United States since 1995. In 2006 Ban, together with architect Dean Maltz, collaborated on the design of a modernist house at Sagaponac, a residential development of thirty-four houses on Long Island, New York.

Furniture House 5 is based on the plan of Mies van der Rohe's unbuilt Brick Country House, conceived in the 1920s and reinterpreted here in wood. It is similar to other houses in the series in that the factory-produced units serve as both structural and space-defining elements. The modular, floor-to-ceiling furniture units, 2.7 m (9 ft) in height, also provide extra storage. During the build, the units worked as a flexible system, with each one light enough for two workers to move, position and install. A total of 144 units were used, including closets, bookcases, linen cupboards, a pantry, partitions and HVAC units. With the house pre-finished inside and out, all that was needed was additional exterior sheathing for waterproofing and insulation.

Following the organizational style and circulation of Mies's floorplan, the spatial concept of Ban and Maltz's design divides the house into four separate zones, enhanced by an individual garden that integrates the interior with the surrounding landscape. The large, glazed façades of the living spaces also contribute to the continuity between the indoors and outside. Each corner is reinforced with triangular pieces of plywood, which bear the horizontal and vertical loads and prevent buckling, and allow the house to have large cantilevers.

The collaboration between Ban and Maltz has produced a modern home that envisions a flexible, efficient space, which allows furniture units to divide the space while simultaneously acting as structural elements. Furniture House 5 is a sequence of spaces, transitions and continuous relationships between the interior and exterior architectural moments; much the same as Mies's Brick Country House. This project demonstrates the successful integration of modular units into a well-organized plan for comfortable living.

The design is based on the plan of Mies van der Rohe's Brick Country House, conceived in the 1920s and reinterpreted here in wood.

Left
Living area.

Below
Hallway.

Opposite, left and right
Bathroom.

Previous pages
View of patio area.

Pre-fabricated additions offer a simple, affordable option for homeowners who find themselves needing more space. Along with enabling families to stay put, additions also have the potential to increase density in urban areas as rental units, or to provide alternative live/work spaces. Adding to an existing home is a more environmentally sustainable practice than building from scratch: the pre-fabrication process reduces the build time and impact on site, and allows the possibility of adding technologies in the future that will save both money and energy.

ADDITIONS

Logistical challenges

Pre-fab additions bring numerous advantages to homeowners, from cost-savings and increased square footage to ease of construction and less material waste. With these benefits, however, comes a series of logistical challenges, including successful installation and resolving the connection between new and old.

Additions can be placed next to or on top of an existing structure. With the former, it is important to ensure that the intersecting roofs shed water and snow properly.[64] A sufficient foundation structure must also be in place. According to the Canada Mortgage and Housing Corporation, this type of addition is less likely to be met with opposition from neighbours, because it will not significantly alter the character of the area.

In the case of vertical additions, the load-bearing capacity of the existing building must be considered, along with connections for heat, electricity and water, which can be more complicated. Chimneys also need to be accommodated. This type of addition, especially if large in scale, has more potential to drastically alter the streetscape, so it is important that the proposed design is visually proportionate with the original building.[65]

Material choices

Since pre-fab additions usually arrive and are placed on site by crane, it is essential that lightweight materials are used. These can include panels, steel frames, composite wood and hybrid systems, all of which result in faster build times and lower costs. Structurally insulated panels, or SIPs, one of the most common pre-fabricated products, are used for walls, floors and roofs. Outer panels, usually made from OSB, contain the inner insulating core material – usually expanded or extruded polystyrene (EPS or XPS), or rigid polyurethane foam – sandwiched between them.

Recycled and reused materials are generally used in modular and pre-fab constructions to increase sustainability, with green-building certifications such as LEED, among others, encouraging more widespread use. Among the most frequently used are gypsum wallboard, cellulose or fibreglass insulation, and exterior sheathing, as well as fill, concrete, roofing, carpet underlay, and more.[66]

Preparation and connection

There are three phases associated with the preparation and connection of pre-fab additions: research and design; demolition and construction of the exterior; and finishing the interior. The design phase begins with studying existing city by-laws and regulations, which can dictate the size and type of addition permitted. The designer must be careful to ensure that the addition complements the existing building, and decisions concerning form, size, materials, colours and façade features also play an important role.[67]

Once the design phase is complete, demolition and construction can begin. Pre-fab additions are built in the factory, using either a panellized or modular system, before being transported to site. Before an addition is craned into position, the excavation and foundation must be completed (in the case of an adjacent addition) or the existing roof demolished and removed (in the case of a vertical one). Once in place, a new roof for the complete structure is built and exterior detailing performed to ensure weather-tight connections. Circulation between the existing building and the new addition must also be provided in the form of a stairwell or hallway.[68]

The third phase involves completing the interior and making it liveable, including connecting the heating, plumbing and electrics, and ensuring there is adequate ventilation. Depending on the level of work performed in the factory, finishing details may still need to be added, including drywalling, painting, millwork, flooring and cabinetry – before the addition is finally complete and ready to be lived in.

Above
**Focus House, UK,
Bere Architects.**

hangers on

Rucksack House
Leipzig, Germany
Stefan Eberstadt

Rucksack House by artist and designer Stefan Eberstadt combines art and architecture to provide form and function, while addressing issues of mobility and flexibility. It is suspended from steel cables – much like a backpack, or rucksack – which are anchored to the roof or façade of a building, allowing the floor space of an individual apartment to be increased. It is transportable, and can be taken to another location when the residents decide to move on.

The extended volume is designed to provide plenty of natural light, and a spacious, open plan that can be adapted to suit different residents. Once inside, the extension feels private and enclosed, although it is clearly apparent from the outside that it is essentially 'floating' beyond the host building, above the public streetscape below. It is on show for everyone to see, but can only be accessed through the apartment.

This particular prototype is 2.5 × 3.6 × 2.5 m (8 × 12 × 8 ft), weighing over 1,600 kg (3,500 lbs), and has a steel frame with a birch-veneered plywood cladding on the inside. Each surface plane – floors, ceilings and walls – has transparent Plexiglas inserts, providing views to the outside and even to the ground below. Cleverly designed and efficient storage allows the 'rucksack' to be used for a variety of living situations, with fold-down furnishings and built-in openings that provide extra space and allow natural light to enter. Sections of the walls, held in place with magnets, unfold into a desk, shelves and a sleeping platform.

Rucksack House combines art and architecture to provide form and function, while addressing issues of mobility and flexibility.

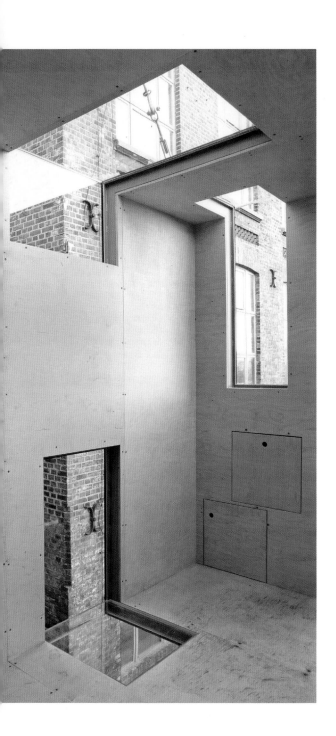

Outside, the cladding is made from exterior-grade plywood, with an absorbent resin surface punctuated by the window slots. The simple, weatherproofed exterior gives the addition a long lifespan and makes it low maintenance, while the pre-fabricated construction method ensures that it can be transported.

Unlike single-family homes, multi-level residential buildings cannot be easily expanded and are not very flexible when it comes to adapting to their residents' changing lifestyles. Although Rucksack House is limited in size, it does allow for expansion to a certain extent and is reusable. With the high housing costs associated with city living, it offers an effective temporary means of gaining more floor space. Stefan Eberstadt's design demonstrates the potential in creating a usable, flexible, multi-purpose space when a permanent solution is not available.

Left
Interior view.

Opposite
Side view of existing building and addition.

lightness of being

XS Extension
Saint-Didier-au-Mont-d'Or, France
Playtime Agence d'Architecture

The idea of designing and constructing an extension to contain a comfortable kitchen and living area is relatively straightforward. For this large 19th-century house in France, however, the architects were challenged with the task of extending the building to complement the historic character of the house without imitating it. The team at Playtime Agence d'Architecture, therefore, delivered a small metallic volume that is inserted between two existing trees, slotting neatly into the landscape.

The extension is a simple, balanced volume, with clean, minimalist lines. It runs parallel to the main building and is fully open on the east and west façades, but entirely closed on the south to prevent overheating. It is positioned as close as possible to one of the trees, with a projecting balcony that is accessible from the kitchen. To make the space as open as possible, the framework was designed with identical angles and lengths in the upper, lower and lateral sections, freeing up a threshold between the interior and exterior of the lower section.

This contemporary addition evokes the feeling of treehouses, wood cabins, mountain refuges, garden pavilions and follies, with the inside merging seamlessly into the outdoors through the glazed façades, framing views of the beautiful landscape. Although XS Extension is a simple construction, there is no doubt that it was built with careful attention to detail. The structure is raised on piles and cantilevers to increase the feeling of lightness and ensure that there is minimal impact on the ground. This separation maintains the relationship

with the main house, with the kitchen acting as a visual 'hyphen' between them and providing views of the garden. The almost exclusive use of metal gives a smooth texture, which contributes to the lightweight feel and reflects the colours of the gently sloping landscape, set within in a grove of hundred-year-old trees with views of the Monts du Lyonnais.

XS Extension was built mainly with dry construction methods, using pre-fabricated metal components. The concrete foundation allows the structure to be cantilevered, with four columns, clad in stainless steel, forming the piles and positioned as close as possible to the house. To preserve the lightness of the addition, the insulation was integrated into the laminated galvanized steel. Shaping was done in the workshop and adjusted on site. The structure is finished with a composite floor, insulation and underfloor heating. Other systems, including a green roof and external insulation, were used to enhance its environmental credentials.

The architects not only designed the building, but also fitted the furniture to ensure that every detail was correct. The result is user-friendly, comprising a limited palette of materials to harmonize with the historic house. Using dry construction methods also provided environmental benefits, from lower energy consumption to allowing the structure to be dismantled or transformed.

Left
View of kitchen.

Opposite
Side view of extension.

Previous pages
Front view of existing house and extension.

Opposite
Extension, at night.

Below
Front view of existing house and extension.

in focus

Focus House
London, UK
Bere Architects

This pre-fabricated eco-home was designed by Bere Architects (see also Camden Passivhaus; p. 36), a firm that has gained a reputation through practical experimentation for producing low-carbon buildings. Its main objective was to swap the original large, high-maintenance home for a compact, low-maintenance, energy-saving one that would provide a larger living space for a family of five by adapting the spatial division of a traditional Victorian house to suit modern needs.

From the front, the extension is only 2.8 m (9 ft) wide, expanding to 7 m (23 ft) at the back. The façade is glazed, providing a view from the garden at the rear of the house through to the trees across the street. The ground floor is organized into areas for dining, cooking, working and lounging. On the first-floor landing, an office space projects outwards, forming a porch above the entrance. A short flight of stairs leads up to the master bedroom, with the bathroom a half-level below the office. This upper section can be closed off from the children's bedrooms, with windows carefully placed to reduce any sense of detachment.

The extension was made in Austria, before being transported to London in kit form. Thanks to the cross-laminated timber slabs that form the walls, upper floors and roof slabs, it was erected within a week. The slabs, made from a sustainable material, can span huge distances. The timber shell is externally insulated, so that the thermal mass is on the inside, where it can moderate extremes of temperature and moisture.

Focus House was built to Passivhaus standards, using non-toxic materials to ensure healthy air and water quality. It also includes super-insulation, airtight construction and solar thermal water heating, with heat-recovery ventilation, water filtration and solid-core, cross-laminated timber construction, all of which contribute to the low-carbon footprint. Although the initial choice of material for the cantilevered office space was in-situ concrete, the cost was too high. A member of the team suggested using solid timber panels instead, which would be easier to build with, as well as cost less and be more sustainable. Timber stores carbon dioxide from the atmosphere during the lifetime of the building, thus compensating for the burning of fossil fuels in cutting and transportation.

Bere Architects achieved a sustainable, affordable house that would meet the changing needs of a large family. Without immediate cost savings, the UK construction industry has little incentive for using sustainable products, but committed architects can produce built designs that benefit both the inhabitants and the environment.

The main objective was to swap a large, high-maintenance home for a compact, low-maintenance, energy-saving one.

PLANS

Casa Algarrobo
pp. 13–17

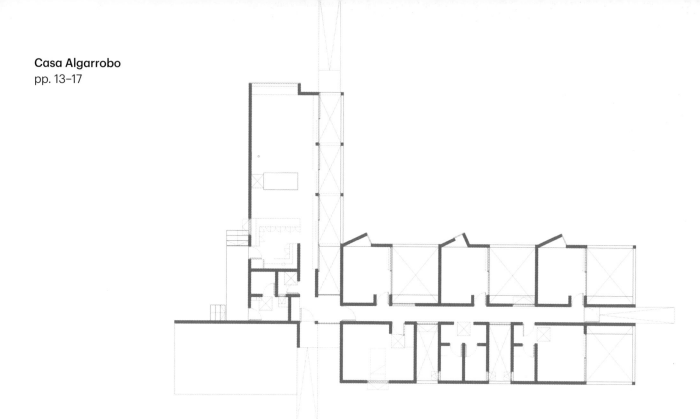

Rubber House
pp. 18–21

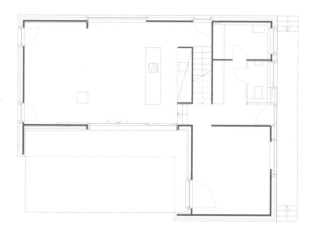

GROUND FLOOR

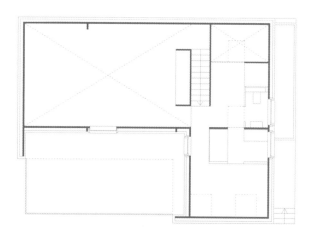

FIRST FLOOR

Happy Cheap House
pp. 22–25

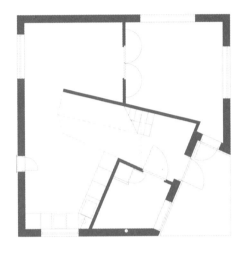

GROUND FLOOR

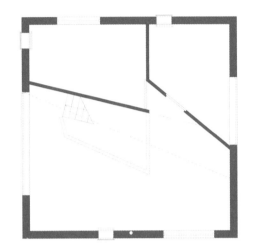

FIRST FLOOR

Living Homes Atwater
pp. 26–29

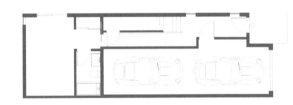

GROUND FLOOR

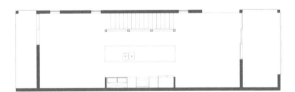

FIRST FLOOR

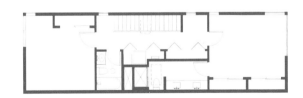

SECOND FLOOR

C3 Pre-fab
pp. 33–35

GROUND FLOOR

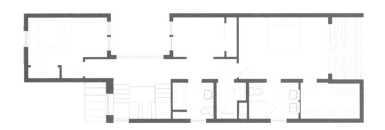

FIRST FLOOR

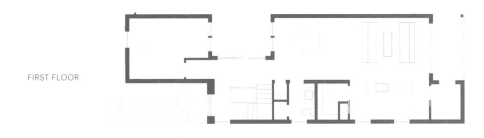

Camden Passivhaus
pp. 36–39

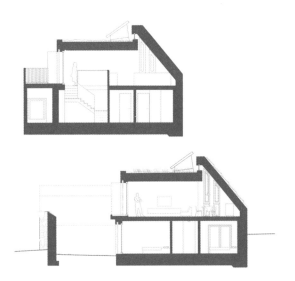

GROUND FLOOR   FIRST FLOOR

Krubiner Residence
pp. 40–43

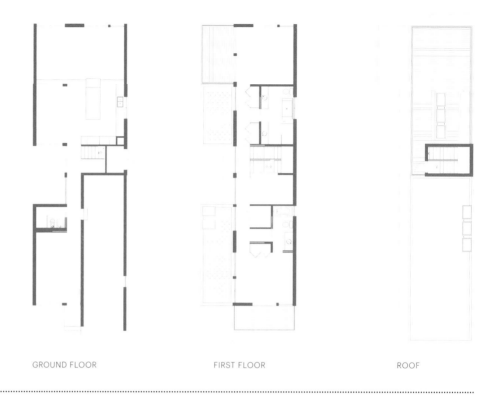

GROUND FLOOR FIRST FLOOR ROOF

57th & Vivian – Solar Laneway House
pp. 44–45

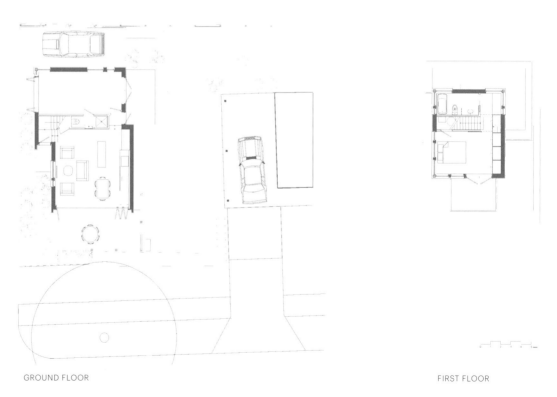

GROUND FLOOR FIRST FLOOR

Y: Cube Mitcham
pp. 49–51

Floating Houses IJburg
pp. 52–55

Town House
pp. 56–61

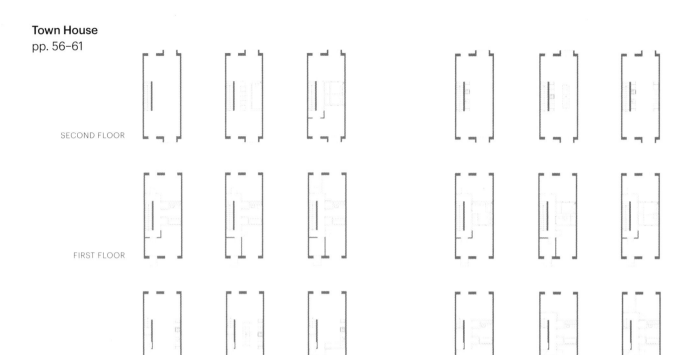

SECOND FLOOR

FIRST FLOOR

GROUND FLOOR

Grow Community
pp. 62–65

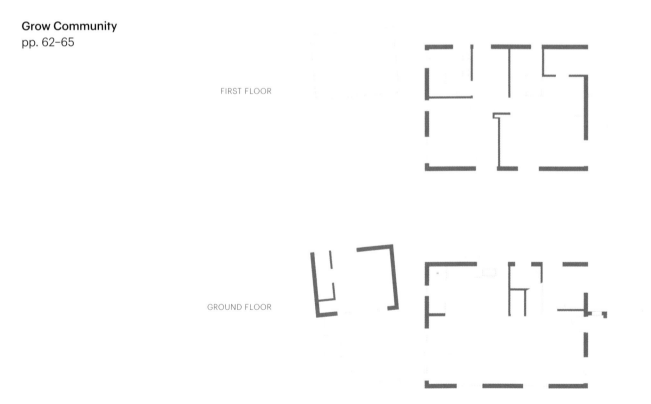

FIRST FLOOR

GROUND FLOOR

House of 33 Years
pp. 69–71

GROUND FLOOR

FIRST FLOOR

A-Ring
pp. 72–75

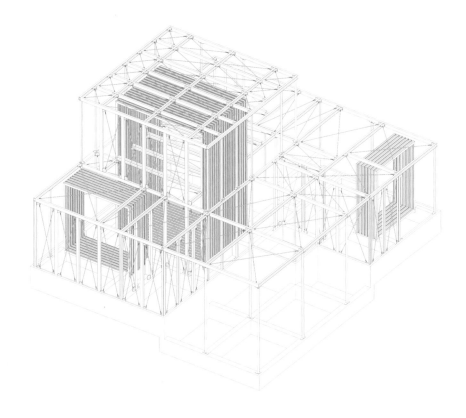

Module Grid House
pp. 76–79

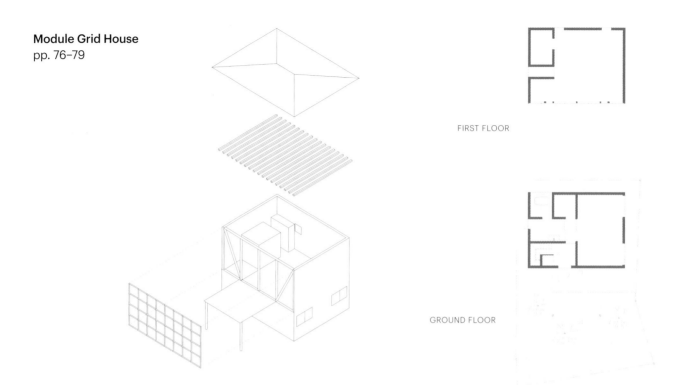

FIRST FLOOR

GROUND FLOOR

Bronx Box
pp. 83–85

FIRST FLOOR

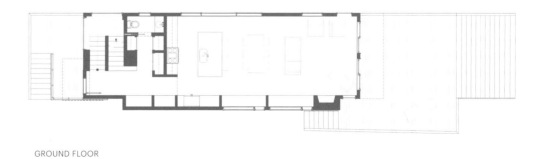

GROUND FLOOR

Small House
pp. 86–87

FIRST FLOOR

GROUND FLOOR

1.8m Width House
pp. 88–93

Collingwood House
pp. 94–95

FIRST FLOOR

GROUND FLOOR

Plus House
pp. 99–103

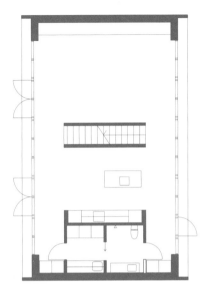

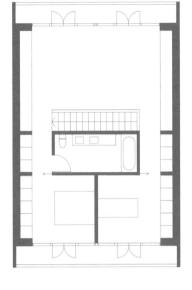

GROUND FLOOR

FIRST FLOOR

Zufferey House
pp. 104–7

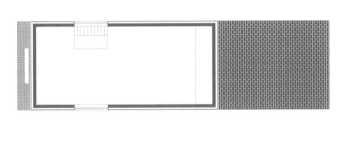

SECOND FLOOR

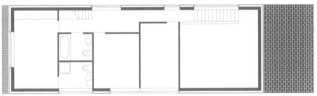

FIRST FLOOR

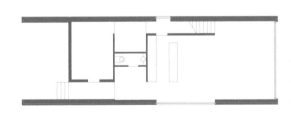

GROUND FLOOR

Casa GG
pp. 108–11

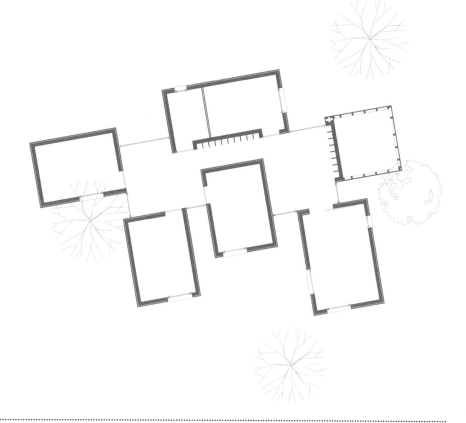

Gambier Island House
pp. 112–15

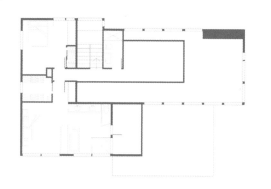

FIRST FLOOR

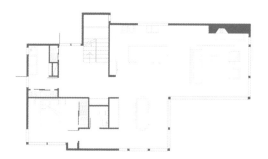

GROUND FLOOR

Loblolly House
pp. 116–21

GROUND FLOOR

FIRST FLOOR

SECOND FLOOR

Heijmans ONE
pp. 125–29

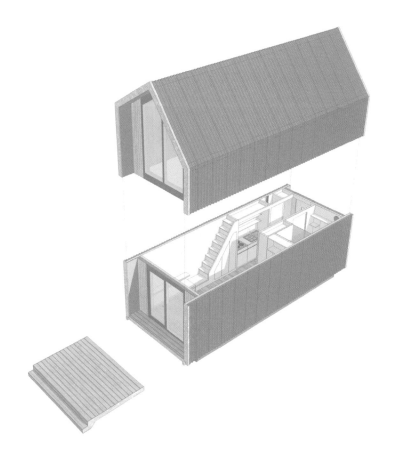

Sonoma weeHouse
pp. 130–35

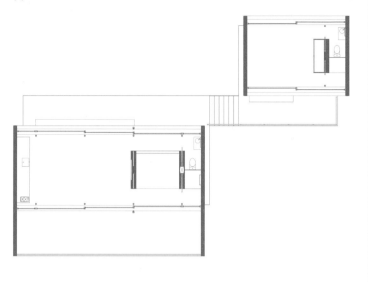

Casa Transportable
pp. 136–41

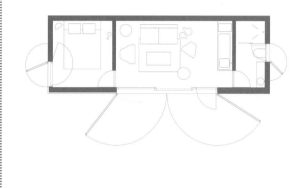

Moho
pp. 145–47

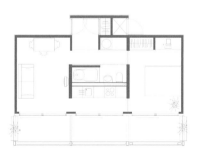

TYPE A

TYPE B

TYPE C

The Stack
pp. 148–51

Containers of Hope
pp. 155–57

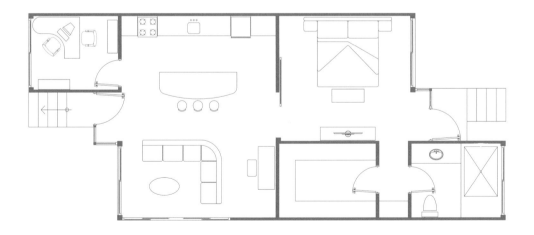

Seatrain
pp. 158–63

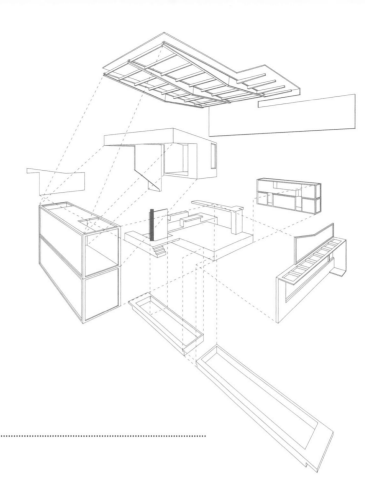

....

Tim Palen Studio at Shadow Mountain
pp. 164–67

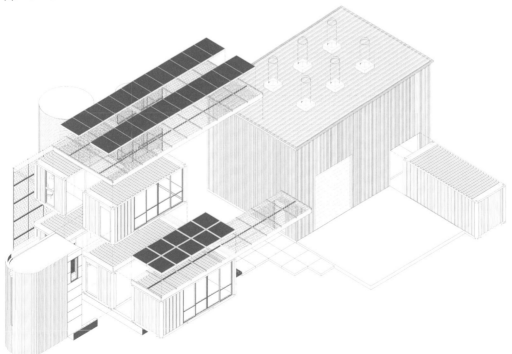

Containerlove
pp. 168–73

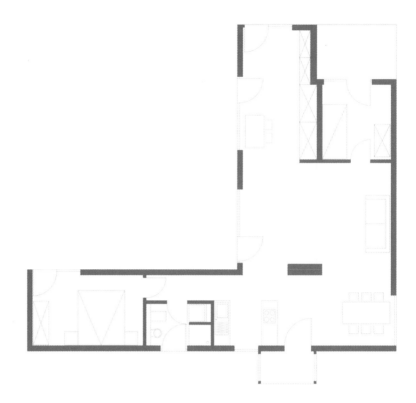

Adaptable House
pp. 177–79

FIRST FLOOR

GROUND FLOOR

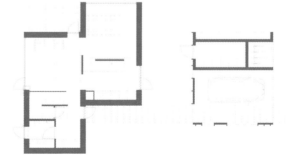

Grid House
pp. 180–85

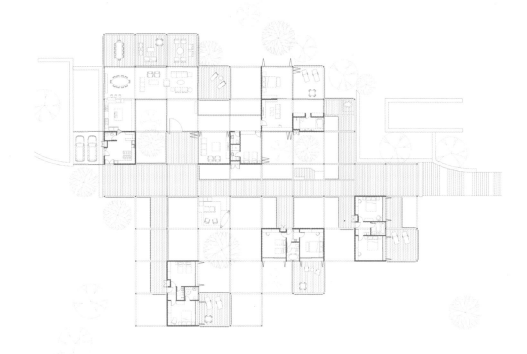

Switch
pp. 186–89

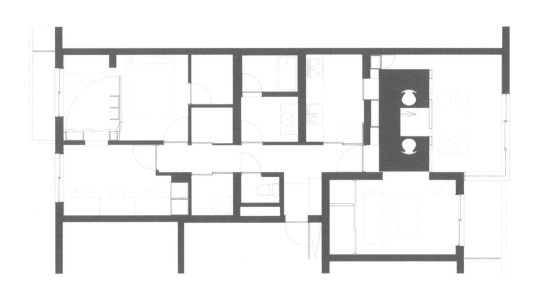

Furniture House 5
pp. 190–93

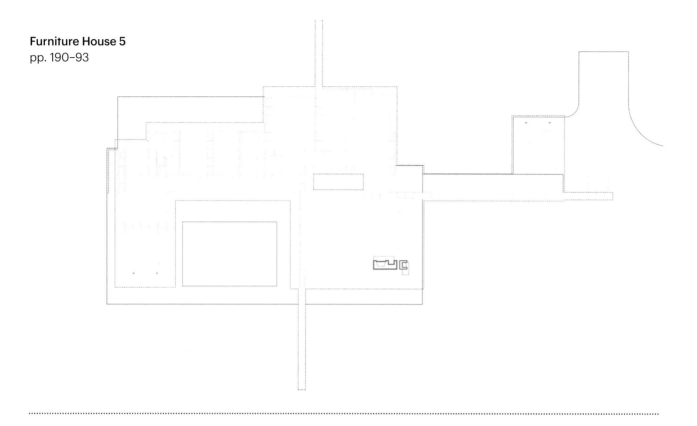

Rucksack House
pp. 197–99

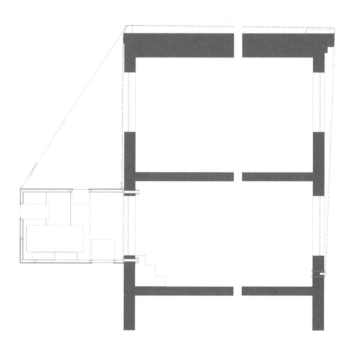

XS Extension
pp. 200–203

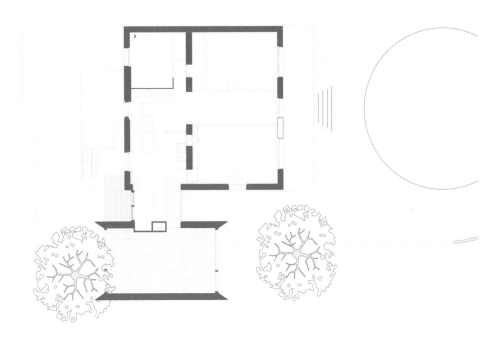

....

Focus House
pp. 204–7

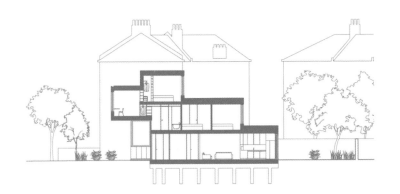

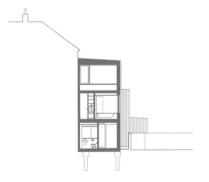

NOTES

1. Modular Homeowners, 'Do you know the difference between prefab and manufactured homes?', 2015. Accessed 9 December 2018. http://modularhomeowners.com/do-you-know-the-difference-between-prefab-and-manufactured-homes.

2. Manufactured Housing Institute, 'Trends and information about the manufactured housing industry', 2016. Accessed 24 May 2017. http://www.manufacturedhousing.org/wp-content/uploads/2016/11/1836temp.pdf.

3. Canadian Mortgage Trends, 'First-time buyers by the numbers', 8 April 2015. Accessed 9 December 2018. http://www.canadianmortgagetrends.com/canadian_mortgage_trends/2015/04/first-time-buyers-by-the-numbers.html.

4. MDPI, 'Material efficiency of building construction', 1 July 2014. Accessed 9 December 2018. https://www.mdpi.com/2075-5309/4/3/266.

5. Trulove, James Grayson, and Ray Cha, *PreFabNow* (New York: Collins Design, 2007).

6. Galindo, Michelle, *Contemporary Prefab Houses* (Salenstein, Switzerland: Braun, 2010).

7. Schneider, Tatjana, and Jeremy Till, *Flexible Housing* (Oxford: Architectural Press, 2007).

8. Autodesk, 'What is BIM?', 2016. Accessed 9 December 2018 http://www.autodesk.com/solutions/bim/overview.

9. Gonchar, Joann, 'Some assembly required', in *Architectural Record* 196:9 (September 2008): 138–46; Trulove and Cha.

10. Davies, Colin, *The Prefabricated Home* (London: Reaktion Books, 2005).

11. Elliott, Monica, 'Adaptable architecture', in *Industrial Engineer* 37:9 (September 2005).

12. Costa Duran, Sergi, *New Prefab Architecture* (Barcelona: Loft Publications, 2008).

13. Torcellini, Paul A., Shanti Pless and Michael Deru, *Zero Energy Buildings: A Critical Look at the Definition* (Washington, DC: National Renewable Energy Laboratory, 2006).

14. Gevorkian, Peter, *Sustainable Energy Systems Engineering: The Complete Green Building Design Resource* (New York: McGraw-Hill Education, 2007).

15. Gevorkian, *Alternative Energy Systems in Building Design* (New York: McGraw-Hill Education, 2008).

16. Tanha, Ali, *Net-Zero Apartment Buildings: Design Strategies and Technologies* (Montreal: McGill University School of Architecture, 2010).

17. Manufactured Housing Institute, 2016.

18. Schneider and Till, 2007.

19. Manufactured Housing Institute, 2016.

20. Pine, B. Joseph, *Mass Customization – The New Frontier in Business Competition* (Boston: Harvard Business School Press, 1993).

21. Noguchi, Masa, *A Choice Model for Mass Customization of Lower-Cost and Higher-Performance Housing in Sustainable Development* (Montreal: McGill University, 2004).

22. Davis Studio Architecture & Design, 'Grow Community', 2014. Accessed 8 December 2018. http://davisstudioad.com/?portfolio=grow-community-2.

23. Noguchi, *User Choice and Flexibility in Japan's Prefabricated Housing Industry: A Case Study* (Montreal: McGill University, 2000).

24. Davies, 2005.

25. Barlow. James G., et al., 'Choice and delivery in house building: lessons from Japan for UK house builders', in *Building Research & Information* 31:2 (January 2003): 134–45.

26. Bergdoll, Barry, and Peter Christensen, *Home Delivery: Fabricating the Modern Dwelling*, exh. cat., Museum of Modern Art, New York, 2008.

27. Noguchi, 2004.

28. Hermanuz, Ghislaine, *Reweaving the Urban Fabric: Approaches to Infill Housing* (New York: New York State Council on the Arts, 1988).

29. Friedman, Avi, *The Grow Home* (Montreal: McGill-Queen's University Press, 2001).

30. Elliot, Lynn, 'Breaking down walls', in *Old House Journal* (El Segundo, California: Active Interest Media, 2002).

31. Friedman, Avi, *Narrow Houses* (New York: Princeton Architectural Press, 2010).

32. Koones, Sheri, *Prefabulous and Almost Off the Grid* (New York: Abrams, 2012).

33. Manufactured Housing Institute, 2016.

34. Koones, 2012.

35. Green Energy Futures, 'The power of passive solar and thermal mass', 10 February 2014. Accessed 25 May 2017. http://www.greenenergyfutures.ca/episode/62-power-passive-solar-and-thermal-mass.

36. Studio Aisslinger, 'LoftCube', 2011. Accessed 28 June 2017. http://www.loftcube.net.

37. Alchemy Architects, 'Process: Frequently asked questions', 2011. Accessed 9 December 2018. http://www.weehouse.com/faq; Studio Aisslinger, 2011.

38. Dornob, 'Portable prefabs: location-independent modular homes', 2011. Accessed 9 December 2018. http://dornob.com/portable-prefabs-location-independent-modular-homes.

39. Melis, Liesbeth, *Parasite Paradise: A Manifesto for Temporary Architecture and Flexible Urbanism* (Rotterdam, Netherlands: NAi Publishers, 2003).

40. Assasi, Reza, *Plug and Play Homes: Self-contained Prefabricated Plug-in Units* (Montreal: McGill University, 2008).

41. Studio Aisslinger, 'Loftcube', 2009. Accessed 9 December 2018. http://www.aisslinger.de/index.php?option=com_project&view=detail&pid=10&Itemid=1.

42. Assasi, 2008.

43. The Globe and Mail, 'Expandable shipping container homes offer adaptable solutions', 2 October 2015. Accessed 29 June 2017. https://www.theglobeandmail.com/real-estate/expandable-shipping-container-homes-offer-adaptable-solutions/article26637516.

44. Wired, 'Plug + play construction', 1 January 2007. Accessed June 29, 2017. https://www.wired.com/2007/01/home1.

45. United Nations, 'World's population increasingly urban with more than half living in urban areas', 10 July 2014. Accessed 9 December 2018. http://www.un.org/en/development/desa/news/population/world-urbanization-prospects-2014.html.

46. Pembina Institute, 'Make way for mid-rise', 2015. Accessed 9 December 2018. https://www.pembina.org/reports/make-way-for-mid-rise.pdf.

47. Linwood Homes, 'Prefab or "prefabulous" – panelized, modular or package home', 2016. Accessed 9 December 2018. http://www.linwoodhomes.com/prefab-or-prefabulous-panelized-modular-or-package-home.

48. Financial Post, 'How factory-built homes are shedding their "cheap" label and exploding in popularity', 20 January 2014. https://business.financialpost.com/personal-finance/mortgages-real-estate/how-factory-built-homes-are-shedding-their-cheap-label-and-exploding-in-popularity.

49. Woodcraft, Saffron, *Design for Social Sustainability: A Framework for Creating Thriving New Communities* (London: The Young Foundation, 2012).

50. Friedman, Avi, *Innovative Houses: Concepts for Sustainable Living* (London: Laurence King Publishing, 2013).

51. Places, 'The emergence of container urbanism', February 2013. Accessed 9 December 2018. https://placesjournal.org/article/the-emergence-of-container-urbanism/?gclid=CjOKCQjwq7XMBRCDARIsAKVI5QZPIMYz4RynArsIrojeY6xgcvOx-6ZdPRC7EDMT5Dlcs4NpLhBBxd8aAhomEALw_wcB#ref_13.

52. Container Solutions, 'ISO specifications', 2015. Accessed 9 December 2018. http://containersolutions.net/specifications.

53. SSAB Weathering, 'Cor-Ten: for extra weather resistance and long life', 2017. Accessed 9 December 2018. http://www.ssab.ca/products/brands/ssab-weathering-steel/products/cor-ten.

54. Western Container Sales, 'Buy shipping containers online', 2016. Accessed 9 December 2018. https://westerncontainersales.com/buy-shipping-containers-online.

55. Places, 2013.

56. Slawik, Han, et al., *Container Atlas: A Practical Guide to Container Architecture* (Berlin: Die Gestalten Verlag, 2010).

57. Knaack, Ulrich, Sharon Chung-Klatte, and Reinhard Hasselbach, *Prefabricated Systems: Principles of Construction* (Basel: Birkhäuser, 2012).

58. Vanier Institute, 'Changing families, new understandings', June 2011. Accessed 9 December 2018. http://vanierinstitute.ca/wp-content/uploads/2015/12/CFT_2011-06-00_EN.pdf.

59. Lawlor, Drue, and Michael A. Thomas, *Residential Design for Aging in Place* (New Jersey: John Wiley & Sons, 2008).

60. Friedman, *The Adaptable House: Designing Homes for Change* (New York: McGraw-Hill Education, 2002).

61. Your Home, 'The livable and adaptable house', 2010. Accessed 9 December 2018. http://www.yourhome.gov.au/sites/prod.yourhome.gov.au/files/pdf/YOURHOME-Housing-TheLivableAndAdaptableHouse.pdf.

62. Friedman, 2002.

63. Conran, Terence, *Small Spaces: Inspiring Ideas and Creative Solutions* (New York: Clarkson Potter, 2001).

64. Gianino, Andrew, *The Modular Home* (North Adams, Massachusetts: Storey Publishers, 2005).

65. Professional Builder, 'Four expandable house design concepts', 18 March 2011. Accessed 9 December 2018. https://www.probuilder.com/4-expandable-house-design-concepts.

66. United States Green Building Council, 'List of common recyclable materials and recycled-content building products', 2017. Accessed 9 December 2018. http://www.usgbc.org.

67. Friedman, 2001.

68. Modular Home Additions, 'The process', 2017. Accessed 9 December 2018. http://www.modular.ca/about-us/the-process.aspx.

BIBLIOGRAPHY

Assasi, Reza, *Plug and Play Homes: Self-contained Prefabricated Plug-in Units* (Montreal: McGill University, 2008).

Barlow, James G., et al., 'Choice and delivery in house building: lessons from Japan for UK house builders', *Building Research & Information* 31:2 (January 2003): 134–45.

Bergdoll, Barry, and Peter Christensen, *Home Delivery: Fabricating the Modern Dwelling*, exh. cat., Museum of Modern Art, New York, 2008.

Conran, Terence, *Small Spaces: Inspiring Ideas and Creative Solutions* (New York: Clarkson Potter, 2001).

Costa Duran, Sergi, *New Prefab Architecture* (Barcelona: Loft Publications, 2008).

Davies, Colin, *The Prefabricated Home* (London: Reaktion Books, 2005).

Elliot, Lynn, 'Breaking down walls', *Old House Journal* (El Segundo, California: Active Interest Media, 2002).

Elliott, Monica, 'Adaptable architecture', *Industrial Engineer* 37:9 (September 2005).

Friedman, Avi, *The Adaptable House: Designing Homes for Change* (New York: McGraw-Hill Education, 2002).

-----, *The Grow Home* (Montreal: McGill-Queen's University Press, 2001).

-----, *Innovative Houses: Concepts for Sustainable Living* (London: Laurence King Publishing, 2013).

-----, *Narrow Houses* (New York: Princeton Architectural Press, 2010).

Galindo, Michelle, *Contemporary Prefab Houses* (Salenstein, Switzerland: Braun, 2010).

Gevorkian, Peter, *Alternative Energy Systems in Building Design* (New York: McGraw-Hill Education, 2008).

-----, *Sustainable Energy Systems Engineering: The Complete Green Building Design Resource* (New York: McGraw-Hill Education, 2007).

Gianino, Andrew, *The Modular Home* (North Adams, Massachusetts: Storey Publishers, 2005).

Gonchar, Joann, 'Some assembly required', *Architectural Record* 196:9 (September, 2008): 138–46.

Hermanuz, Ghislaine, *Reweaving the Urban Fabric: Approaches to Infill Housing* (New York: New York State Council on the Arts, 1988).

Knaack, Ulrich, Sharon Chung-Klatte, and Reinhard Hasselbach, *Prefabricated Systems: Principles of Construction* (Basel: Birkhäuser, 2012).

Koones, Sheri, *Prefabulous and Almost Off the Grid* (New York: Abrams, 2012).

Lawlor, Drue, and Michael A. Thomas, *Residential Design for Aging in Place* (New Jersey: John Wiley & Sons, 2008).

Melis, Liesbeth, *Parasite Paradise: A Manifesto for Temporary Architecture and Flexible Urbanism* (Rotterdam, Netherlands: NAi Publishers, 2003).

Noguchi, Masa, *A Choice Model for Mass Customization of Lower-Cost and Higher-Performance Housing in Sustainable Development* (Montreal: McGill University, 2004).

-----, *User Choice and Flexibility in Japan's Prefabricated Housing Industry: A Case Study* (Montreal: McGill University, 2000).

Pine, B. Joseph, *Mass Customization – The New Frontier in Business Competition* (Boston: Harvard Business School Press, 1993).

Rey, Emmanuel, *From Spatial Development to Detail* (Lucerne: Quart Publishers, 2015).

Schneider, Tatjana, and Jeremy Till, *Flexible Housing* (Oxford: Architectural Press, 2007).

Slawik, Han, et al., *Container Atlas: A Practical Guide to Container Architecture* (Berlin: Die Gestalten Verlag, 2010).

Stevenson, Katherine Cole, and H. Ward Jandl, *Houses by Mail: A Guide to Houses by Sears, Roebuck and Company* (Lafayette, Louisiana: Preservation Press, 1986).

Tanha, Ali, *Net-Zero Apartment Buildings: Design Strategies and Technologies* (Montreal: McGill University School of Architecture, 2010).

Torcellini, Paul A., Shanti Pless and Michael Deru, *Zero Energy Buildings: A Critical Look at the Definition* (Washington, DC: National Renewable Energy Laboratory, 2006).

Trulove, James Grayson, and Ray Cha, *PreFabNow* (New York: Collins Design, 2007).

Winchip, Susan M., *Sustainable Design for Interior Environments* (New York: Fairchild Publications, 2007).

Woodcraft, Saffron, *Design for Social Sustainability: A Framework for Creating Thriving New Communities* (London: The Young Foundation, 2012).

DIRECTORY

Ábaton Arquitectura (p. 136)
Calle Cdad. Real, 28, 28223 Pozuelo de Alarcón,
Madrid, Spain
abaton.es

Alchemy Architects (p. 130)
856 Raymond Avenue, Suite G,
St Paul, Minnesota 55114, USA
weehouse.com

Alventosa Morell Arquitectes (p. 108)
Carrer de Rocafort, 67, 08015 Barcelona, Spain
alventosamorell.com

ArchiBlox (p. 94)
Studio 5, 149–151 Barkly Avenue,
Richmond, Victoria, Australia
archiblox.com.au

Assistant (p. 69)
3-53-11-205 Sendagaya, Shibuya, Tokyo, Japan
withassistant.net

Atelier Tekuto (p. 72)
4 Chome-1-20 Jingumae,
Shibuya, Tokyo 150-0001, Japan
tekuto.com

Shigeru Ban and Dean Maltz (p. 190)
330 West 38th Street, Suite 811,
New York, New York 10018, USA
shigerubanarchitects.com
dma-ny.com

Bauart Architekten (p. 86)
Zimmerlistraße 6,8004 Zürich, Switzerland
bauart.ch

Bere Architects (pp. 36, 204)
54a Newington Green, London N16 9PX, UK
bere.co.uk

Tommy Carlsson Arkitektur (p. 22)
Åsögatan 119, 116 24 Stockholm, Sweden
tommycarlssonarkitektur.se

Cityförster (p. 18)
Charloisse Kerksingel 14,
NL-3082 DA Rotterdam, Germany
cityfoerster.net

Claesson Koivisto Rune (p. 99)
Östgötagatan 50, 116 64 Stockholm, Sweden
claessonkoivistorune.se

Davis Studio (p. 62)
310 Madison Ave S.,
Bainbridge Island, Washington 98110, USA
davisstudioad.com

Stefan Eberstadt (p. 197)
Parkweg 1, 85305 Jetzendorf, Germany
stefaneberstadt.de

Ecotech Design (p. 164)
8834 W. Hollywood Hills Road,
Los Angeles, California 90046, USA
ecotechdesign.com

FGMF Arquitetos (p. 180)
R. Auriflama, 61, Pinheiros,
São Paulo, 05422-080, Brazil
fgmf.com.br

GA Estudio (p. 13)
Merced 188, Lastarria, Santiago, Chile
garquitectos.cl

Gluck+ (p. 148)
23 West 127th Street, #6,
New York, New York 10027, USA
gluckplus.com

KieranTimberlake (p. 116)
841 N. American Street,
Philadelphia, Pennsylvania 19123, USA
kierantimberlake.com

Lanefab Design/Build (p. 44)
362 East 10th Avenue,
Vancouver, BC V5T 1Z7, Canada
lanefab.com

Henning Larsen and GXN (p. 177)
Vesterbrogade 76, 1620 Copenhagen V, Denmark
henninglarsen.com
Kanonbådsvej 8, 1437 Copenhagen K, Denmark
3xn.com

LHVH Architekten (p. 168)
Heinrich-Rohlmann-Straße 10,
50829 Cologne, Germany
lhvh.de

Living Homes (p. 26)
375 S. Cactus Avenue,
Rialto, California 92376, USA
livinghomes.net

MoodBuilders (p. 125)
Klokgebouw 144, 5617 AB Eindhoven
nr 144-21, Netherlands
mood-builders.com

Nunatak Architectes (p. 104)
Rue des Follatères 15, 1926 Fully, Valais, Switzerland
nunatak.ch

Office of Mobile Design (p. 158)
1725 Abbot Kinney Boulevard,
Los Angeles, California 90291, USA
designmobile.com

Playtime Agence d'Architecture (p. 200)
37, rue Pierre Dupont, 69001 Lyon, France
playtimearchitecture.com

Resolution: 4 Architecture (p. 83)
150 West 28th Street, Suite 1902,
New York, New York 10001, USA
re4a.com

Rogers Stirk Harbour & Partners (p. 49)
122 Leadenhall Street, London EC3V 4AB, UK
rsh-p.com

Marlies Rohmer (p. 52)
Kerkstraat 204, 1017 GV Amsterdam, Netherlands
rohmer.nl

Benjamin Garcia Saxe (p. 155)
P.O. Box 206-1225, San Jose, Costa Rica
studiosaxe.com

ShedKM (pp. 56, 145)
115 Golden Lane, London EC1Y 0TJ, UK
shedkm.co.uk

Yuko Shibata Office (p. 186)
302 Nozawamyrtlecourt, 2-8-16 Nozawa,
Tokyo 154-0003, Japan
yukoshibata.com

Square Root (p. 33)
4656 North Leclaire Avenue,
Chicago, Illinois 60630, USA
squarerootarch.com

Swatt/Miers Architects (p. 40)
5845 Doyle Street, #104,
Emeryville, California 94608, USA
swattmiers.com

Turkel Design (p. 112)
840 Summer Street, #104,
Boston, Massachusetts 02127, USA
turkeldesign.com

Tetsuo Yamaji Architects (p. 76)
6 Chome–3–6 Nishigotanda,
Shinagawa, Tokyo 141-0031, Japan
ymja.jp

YUUA Architects (p. 88)
4 Chome-45-9 Koenjikita,
Suginami, Tokyo 166-0002, Japan
yuua.jp

PROJECT CREDITS

1.8m Width House (p. 88)
Toshima, Japan
Architect: YUUA Architects
Area: 80 m² (861 sq ft)
Completed: 2012

57th & Vivian –
Solar Laneway House (p. 44)
Vancouver, British Columbia, Canada
Architect: Lanefab Design/Build
Area: 95 m² (1,023 sq ft)
Completed: 2012

Adaptable House (p. 177)
Nyborg, Denmark
Architect: Henning Larsen and GXN
Area: 146 m² (1,572 sq ft)
Completed: 2013

A-Ring (p. 72)
Ishikawa, Japan
Architect: Atelier Tekuto
Area: 137 m² (1,471 sq ft)
Completed: 2009

Bronx Box (p. 83)
New York, New York, USA
Architect: Resolution: 4 Architecture
Area: 169 m² (1,816 sq ft)
Completed: 2008

C3 Pre-fab (p. 33)
Chicago, Illinois, USA
Architect: Square Root
Area: 189 m² (2,039 sq ft)
Completed: 2011

Camden Passivhaus (p. 36)
London, UK
Architect: Bere Architects
Area: 101 m² (1,087 sq ft)
Completed: 2010

Casa Algarrobo (p. 13)
Algarrobo, Chile
Architect: GA Estudio
Area: 160 m² (1,722 sq ft)
Completed: 2015

Casa GG (p. 108)
Santa Maria de Palautordera, Spain
Architect: Alventosa Morell
Arquitectes
Area: 111 m² (1,195 sq ft)
Completed: 2013

Casa Transportable (p. 136)
Spain
Architect: Ábaton Arquitectura
Area: 27 m² (291 sq ft)

Collingwood House (p. 94)
Melbourne, Victoria, Australia
Architect: ArchiBlox
Area: 70 m² (753 sq ft)

Containerlove (p. 168)
Kall, Germany
Architect: LHVH Architekten
Area: 90 m² (969 sq ft)
Completed: 2006

Containers of Hope (p. 155)
San Jose, Costa Rica
Architect: Benjamin Garcia Saxe
Area: 100 m² (1,076 sq ft)
Completed: 2011

Floating Houses IJburg (p. 52)
Amsterdam, Netherlands
Architect: Marlies Rohmer
Area: 142 m² (1,529 sq ft)
Completed: 2011

Focus House (p. 204)
London, UK
Architect: Bere Architects
Area: 250 m² (2,961 sq ft)
Completed: 2007

Furniture House 5 (p. 190)
Long Island, New York, USA
Architect: Shigeru Ban and Dean Maltz
Completed: 2006

Gambier Island House (p. 112)
Gambier Island, BC, Canada
Architect: Turkel Design
Area: 231 m² (2,490 sq ft)
Completed: 2008

Grid House (p. 180)
Minas Gerais, Brazil
Architect: FGMF Arquitetos
Area: 3,123 m² (33,615 sq ft)
Completed: 2008

Grow Community (p. 62)
Bainbridge Island, Washington, USA
Architect: Davis Studio
Area: from 107 m² (1,155 sq ft)
Completed: 2014

Happy Cheap House (p. 22)
Stockholm, Sweden
Architect: Tommy Carlsson Arkitektur
Area: 110 m² (1,185 sq ft)
Completed: 2014

Heijmans ONE (p. 125)
Amsterdam, Netherlands
Architect: MoodBuilders
Area: 45 m² (484 sq ft)

House of 33 Years (p. 69)
Nara, Japan
Architect: Assistant
Area: 104 m² (1,119 sq ft)
Completed: 2013

Krubiner Residence (p. 40)
Emeryville, California, USA
Architect: Swatt/Miers Architects
Area: 232 m² (2,500 sq ft)
Completed: 2012

Living Homes Atwater (p. 26)
Los Angeles, California, USA
Architect: Living Homes
Area: 110 m² (1,185 sq ft)
Completed: 2011

Loblolly House (p. 116)
Taylors Island, Maryland, USA
Architect: KieranTimberlake
Area: 204 m² (2,200 sq ft)
Completed: 2006

Module Grid House (p. 76)
Saitama, Japan
Architects: Tetsuo Yamaji Architects
Area: 208 m² (2,239 sq ft)
Completed: 2015

Moho (p. 145)
Manchester, UK
Architect: ShedKM
Area: 3,400 m² (36,597 sq ft)

Plus House (p. 99)
Tyresö, Sweden
Architect: Claesson Koivisto Rune
Area: 162 m² (1,750 sq ft)
Completed: 2007

Rubber House (p. 18)
Almere, Netherlands
Architect: Cityförster
Area: 125 m² (1,345 sq ft)
Completed: 2011

Rucksack House (p. 197)
Leipzig, Germany
Architect: Stefan Eberstadt
Area: 9 m² (97 sq ft)
Completed: 2004

Seatrain (p. 158)
Los Angeles, California, USA
Architect: Office of Mobile Design
Area: 279 m² (3,000 sq ft)

Smallhouse (p. 86)
Switzerland
Architect: Bauart Architekten
Area: 75 m² (807 sq ft)

Sonoma weeHouse (p. 130)
Santa Rosa, California, USA
Architect: Alchemy Architects
Area: 59.4 m² (640 sq ft) + 30.6 m²
(330 sq ft)

The Stack (p. 148)
New York, New York, USA
Architect: Gluck+v
Area: 3,530 m² (38,000 sq ft)

Switch (p. 186)
Tokyo, Japan
Architect: Yuko Shibata Office
Area: 87 m² (940 sq ft)
Completed: 2010

Tim Palen Studio at
Shadow Mountain (p. 164)
San Bernardino, California, USA
Architect: Ecotech Design
Area: 214 m² (2,300 sq ft)

Town House (p. 56)
Manchester, UK
Architect: ShedKM
Area: 26 m² (280 sq ft)
Completed: 2016

XS Extension (p. 200)
Saint-Didier-au-Mont-d'Or, France
Architect: Playtime Agence
d'Architecture
Area: 45 m² (484 sq ft)
Completed: 2015

Y: Cube Mitcham (p. 49)
London, UK
Architect: Rogers Stirk Harbour &
Partners
Area: 26 m² (280 sq ft)
Completed: 2015

Zufferey House (p. 104)
Valais, Switzerland
Architect: Nunatak Architectes
Area: 182 m² (1,959 sq ft)
Completed: 2003

PHOTO CREDITS & ACKNOWLEDGMENTS

All plans and drawings supplied courtesy of the architects.
t = top; b = bottom; l = left; r = right

2 Roos Aldershoff; **6–7** Peter Aaron/Otto; **8** Keith Baker Photography; **12** Avi Friedman; **13–17** Sebastián Aedo; **18–21** Arne Hansen, Nils Nolting; **22–5** © Michael Perlmutter; **26–9** Jo David; **32** Tim Crocker; **33–5** Mike Schwartz Photography (mikeschwartzphoto.com); **36–9** Tim Crocker; **40–3** Russell Abraham Photography; **45** Dylan Doubt; **48** © Luuk Kramer; **49** Morley von Sternberg; **50–1** Rogers Stirk Harbour & Partners; **52–3** Roos Aldershoff; **54t** Marcel van der Burg; **54b** © Matteo Rossi; **55** Ton van Namen; **56–7** © Felix Mooneeram; **58–59** © Jack Hobhouse; **60l** © Felix Mooneeram; **60–61r** © Urban Splash; **62–4** © David W. Cohen Photography; **65** Davis Studio Architecture & Design; **68** Toshihiro Sobajima; **69–71** © Shinkenchiku Sha; **72–5** Toshihiro Sobajima; **76–9** Kenta Hasegawa; **82** Avi Friedman; **83** © RES4; **84, 85** © Laurie Lambrecht; **86–7** © Bauart Architekten und Planer AG; **88–93** Toshihiro Sobajima; **95** Tom Ross; **98** Avi Friedman; **99–103** Åke Eison Lindman; **104–7** Dominique Marc Wehrli; **108–11** Apria Gouca; **112–15** Lindal Cedar Homes; **116–21** Peter Aaron/Otto; **124** © Juan Baraja (www.juanbaraja.com); **125–9** MoodBuilders; **130–5** © Alchemy LLC; **136–41** © Juan Baraja (www.juanbaraja.com); **144** Gluck+; **145** shaw+shaw; **146** © Urban Splash; **147** shaw+shaw; **148–51** Amy Barkow; **154** Jack Parsons Photography; **155–7** Andres Garcia Lachner; **158–63** Daniel Hennessy; **164–7** Jack Parsons Photography; **166–73** Tomas Riehle; **176** © Michael Moran; **177–9** Jesper Ray/Realdania Byg; **180–5** Fotos Rafaela Netto; **186–9** Ryohei Hamada; **190–93** © Michael Moran; **196** Edward Gibbs, Peter Cook, Jefferson Smith; **197–9** © 2004 Stefan Eberstadt, Munich; **200–3** Playtime Architecture – Studio Erick Saillet; **204–7** Edward Gibbs, Peter Cook, Jefferson Smith

Pre-fabricated residential design was a topic of my research and practice for years, and included collaboration with numerous colleagues, assistants and students, who both directly and indirectly inspired the generation of the ideas and the writing of this book.

Mini Cheon played a key role in finding the outstanding projects listed here and describing them. Her dedication, hard work and interest in the subject are much appreciated. I would also like to thank Si Liang (Cicily) Du and Morgan Matheson for their contribution to background research and the writing of the essays. Ben Kennedy was instrumental in helping assemble material from the firms, as well as commenting on and proofreading the text. This book could not have been completed without the hard work, care and attention of Charles Grégoire to processing the project's drawings and photos and readying them for publication. His insightful comments, sharp eye and dedication are highly appreciated. Special thanks to all the design firms and the photographers whose work is featured here.

I would like to express my gratitude to Lucas Dietrich, Fleur Jones and Elain McAlpine at Thames & Hudson, as well as Myfanwy Vernon-Hunt, for ushering the book in, editing and design, and for their patience and guidance in seeing it through. Thanks to the McGill University's School of Architecture, where the genesis of the ideas expressed here began and my own research was carried out. Finally, my heartfelt thanks and appreciation to my wife Sorel Friedman, PhD, and children Paloma and Ben for their love and support.

On the cover: *Front* Casa Transportable ÁPH80, Spain, by Ábaton Arquitectura (photo © Juan Baraja, www.juanbaraja.com); *Back* Sonoma weeHouse, California, by Alchemy Architects (photo © Alchemy LLC)

First published in the United Kingdom in 2021 by Thames & Hudson Ltd, 181A High Holborn, London WC1V 7QX

First published in the United States of America in 2021 by Thames & Hudson Inc., 500 Fifth Avenue, New York, New York 10110

Pre-Fab Living © 2021 Thames & Hudson Ltd
Text © 2021 Avi Friedman

Designed by Myfanwy Vernon-Hunt (this-side.co.uk)

British Library Cataloguing-in-Publication Data
A catalogue record for this book is available from the British Library

Library of Congress Control Number 2020932212

ISBN 978-0-500-34348-7

Printed and bound in China by 1010 Printing International Ltd

Be the first to know about our new releases, exclusive content and author events by visiting
thamesandhudson.com
thamesandhudsonusa.com
thamesandhudson.com.au

Avi Friedman is a professor of architecture at McGill University, Canada, an honorary professor at Lancaster University, UK, and president of Avi Friedman Consultants, Inc., a design firm with a focus on affordable and sustainable residential environments. He has written fourteen books and his design work and projects have been cited in magazines, newspapers and TV shows, including *Good Morning America*, *Dream Builders* and Stewart Brand's *How Buildings Learn*. In 2000, *Wallpaper** included him in their list of ten people 'most likely to change the way we live'.